Toys and Games

DOLLS HOUSE DO-IT-YOURSELF

Toys and Games

Jane Harrop

David & Charles

I would like to dedicate this book to my family and my students, to thank them for their continued support and encouragement.

A DAVID & CHARLES BOOK

First published in the UK in 2003

Copyright © Jane Harrop 2003

Distributed in North America
by F&W Publications, Inc.
4700 East Galbraith Road
Cincinnati, OH 45236
1-800-289-0963

Jane Harrop has asserted her right to be identified as author of this work in accordance with the Copyright, Designs and Patents Act, 1988.

A catalogue record for this book is available from the British Library.

ISBN 0 7153 1436 X paperback

Printed in Hong Kong by Dai Nippon Printing
for David & Charles
Brunel House   Newton Abbot   Devon

Executive Editor Cheryl Brown
Desk Editor Jennifer Proverbs
Executive Art Editor Ali Myer
Senior Designer Prudence Rogers
Production Controller Ros Napper
Copy-editor Linda Clements
Photographer Mark Jarvis

Dolls appearing in chapter opening photographs from
Katy Sue Dolls (see Suppliers)

Visit our website at www.davidandcharles.co.uk

David & Charles books are available from all good bookshops; alternatively you can contact our Orderline on (0)1626 334555 or write to us at FREEPOST EX2110, David & Charles Direct, Newton Abbot TQ12 4ZZ (No stamp required UK mainland).

DOLLS HOUSE DO-IT-YOURSELF

Toys and Games

Contents

Introduction	6	**PARLOUR GAMES**	
Materials and Equipment	8	Table-top Skittles	44
Basic Techniques	12	Table-top Quoits	45
		Indoor Croquet Set	46
TOYS THAT TEACH		Bagatelle	48
Building Blocks	14	Draughts	50
Abacus	15		
Xylophone	16	**OUTDOOR TOYS AND GAMES**	
Picture Bricks	17	Skipping Rope and Hoop	52
Blackboard	18	Windmill	53
Hammer and Pegs	20	Tennis Racket and Ball	54
Rattle	21	Cricket Bat and Ball	55
Paper Toys	22	Go-cart	56
		Kite	58
PUSH AND PULL TOYS		Sailing Boat	60
Rocking Horse	24		
Barrel Horse	26	Templates	61
Sheep on Wheels	28	Suppliers	63
Train Set	30	Acknowledgments	64
Doll's Pram	32	About the author	64
Brick Truck	34	Index	64

DOLLS AND PUPPETS

Toy Theatre	36
Puppet Theatre and Puppets	38
Jack-in-the-Box	40
Doll	42

Introduction

This book aims to guide you through making quality one-twelfth scale toys and games for your dolls' house, through step-by-step instructions and photographs (actual size where possible). While researching old toys, through books and visiting museums, it was fascinating to discover the background of each toy, so each project starts with a short summary of the toy's history and its suitability for the different periods of your dolls' houses.

Up until the middle of the 19th century, only the very rich were able to afford toys made by toymakers, and it was only when toys began to be made in factories that they became cheaper. By the beginning of the 20th century, toyshops had something for everyone – well-made toys for the rich and cheaper toys for the poor. This is why many of the projects described here fall mainly into the Victorian period (1837–1901) and onwards.

I began making miniatures nine years ago and what started as a hobby is now my part-time job: I teach adult education classes on making dolls' house miniatures and also

though everyone has followed the same instructions and used the same materials, each display is different, with each student having their own way of finishing a project and adding ideas of their own. I am sure that this will also happen when you are making up the projects in this book, so don't worry if your item doesn't look exactly like the photograph – remember that all toymakers have their own personal style. Enjoy discovering yours.

sell my work through local miniatures fairs to collectors. Many of the projects in this book have been made by my students, so have been tried and tested!

One of the most rewarding experiences when teaching the miniature courses is the last lesson when each student displays their term's work. It is remarkable that even

Conversion Chart

All the projects in the book are one-twelfth scale, i.e., one inch in miniature is equal to one foot in full size and this is why miniaturists still work to imperial measurements. In general most miniature materials and tools are sold in imperial sizes, although some suppliers are now using metric measurements. The table below provides a guide to converting metric to imperial and vice versa, giving conversions that are relevant to this book. In practice, items may not be sold to their exact equivalent, for example a $1/32$in drill bit is sold in metric as 0.8mm not 0.79mm, so very small degrees of measurement in metric have been rounded up or down.

Inch	Millimetre
$1/64$	0.4
$1/32$	0.8
$3/64$	1.2
$1/16$	1.6
$3/32$	2.4
$1/8$	3.2
$3/16$	4.8
$1/4$	6.3
$3/8$	9.5
$1/2$	12.7
$5/8$	15.9
$3/4$	19.0
$7/8$	22.0
1	25.4

Materials and Equipment

This section describes the basic materials and equipment that you will need to complete the projects. They are readily available from craft and model shops but if you have difficulty in sourcing any of the items refer to Suppliers on page 63. Always read through a project before you begin to ensure that you have the materials and equipment you will require to hand. There is also important safety advice on page 11.

Wood

Many of the projects are made of wood. The type of wood used is stated in each project but can be substituted if desired. Keep to the same wood type during a project for best results.

Bass wood A white-coloured wood with a fine, straight grain. It is harder to cut than obechi but is less likely to split when drilled.

Jelutong wood A straw-coloured wood with a closed grain, ideal for small and detailed woodworking.

Obechi wood A pale yellow-coloured wood with an open grain. It is one of the lightest hardwoods available, making it ideal for sawing and cutting.

Wood dowel Cylindrical wood available in various diameters.

Bass wood

Jelutong wood

Obechi wood

Wood dowel

Tools

These tools wil make working with wood accurate, safe and simple.

Clamps These are ideal for holding wooden components in position whilst glue dries.

Drills Mini electric drills are supplied with a range of fine drill bits. They are more expensive but are quicker than a hand-held pin vice (see below).

Mitre cutters These are basically scissors for wood and will cut and mitre strip wood up to $1/2$in thick. They are used as an alternative to a saw and mitre block.

Pin files These have fine, shaped heads for intricate shaping and sanding.

Pin vice A pin vice is used for drilling through wood and will hold extremely fine drill bits up to $1/8$in diameter.

Sandpaper Essential for shaping, smoothing and distressing wood. Use mostly fine-grade sandpaper for projects at this scale.

Saw and mitre block A junior hacksaw or razor saw are used together with a small mitre block to cut and mitre strip wood. They are used as an alternative to mitre cutters. Use a junior hacksaw and mitre block to cut aluminium tube.

Pin file

Mitre cutters

Saw and mitre block

Clamp

Sandpaper

Pin vice

Colouring Mediums and Glues

Various colouring mediums and glues are used in the projects – see also Basic Techniques, page 12.

Paints Available in a wide range, either water-based or oil-based. Most of the projects use acrylic water-based paints, which are non-toxic and easy to work with. Matt and gloss finishes are available in acrylics. Several of the projects require oil-based spray or enamel paints (see safety tips on page 11).

Paintbrushes Artist's paintbrushes are available in a range of sizes which are ideal for painting miniature toys.

Metallic pastes Wax-based pastes, also known as gilt creams, can be rubbed on to a painted surface to give the appearance of age and depth.

Wood stain A water-based or oil-based colouring applied to wood with a soft cloth (see techniques page 12).

Shoe polish A wax-based wood stain and polish combined (see techniques page 12).

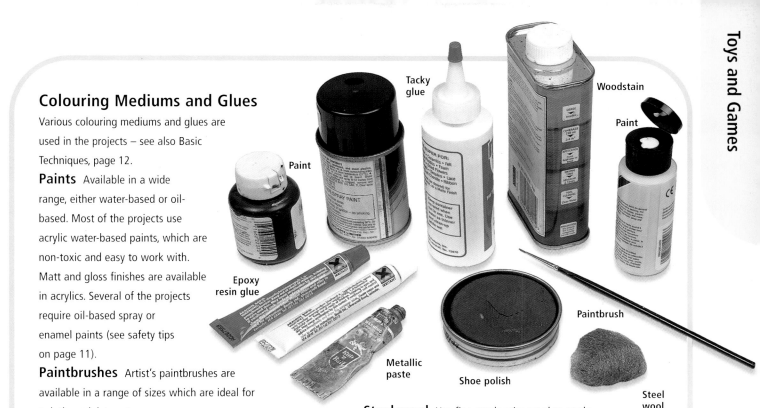

Paint · Tacky glue · Woodstain · Paint · Epoxy resin glue · Metallic paste · Shoe polish · Paintbrush · Steel wool

Steel wool Use fine-grade wire wool to apply shoe polish to wood.

Tacky glue A non-toxic water-based glue that dries strong, clear and flexible. It is particularly suited to wood, paper, card and fabric. Thick or mighty tacky glue is recommended for best results.

Epoxy resin glue A resin-based glue, only used in projects where tacky glue is unsuitable.

Basic Crafting Tools

There are some universal crafting tools that you will find handy for most projects.

Craft knife An essential tool for cutting wood and card. Model maker's knives with replaceable blades are preferable to Stanley knives. Always use with a cutting mat and steel ruler.

Cutting mat A must when cutting with a craft knife to protect working surfaces. Use either a self-healing cutting mat or card that is at least $^{3}/_{32}$in thick.

Ruler A 12in steel ruler graduated in $^{1}/_{16}$in is an essential basic tool.

Scissors Small, sharp scissors are essential for cutting paper and templates.

Paper punches Several of the projects use paper punches, available in a wide variety of shapes and sizes for the craft worker. If you don't wish to go to the expense, similar shapes may be cut out by hand, but obviously the results may not be as precise.

Pliers A useful tool for holding, cutting and bending wire.

Scissors · Metal ruler · Cutting mat · Pliers · Craft knife · Paper punches

Specialist Materials

The list is a useful illustrated glossary and is arranged alphabetically. It features an explanation of all the other items used to complete the projects, some of which may be unfamiliar to you.

Aluminium foil and tape Thin aluminium foil can be cut from food containers. Fine adhesive aluminium tape is available from car accessory shops.

Aluminium tube A hollow tube available in a range of diameters from model shops and cut using a mitre block and junior hacksaw.

Ball bearings Metal balls available in various sizes, often used in model engineering.

Beads Three types of bead are used:

Metal washer beads Used to simulate wheels and available in base metals or plated.

Seed beads Tiny plastic beads, sized according to how many beads fit within an inch when laid in line.

Wooden beads Used in many projects to simulate components such as heads and wheels. When painting use unvarnished wooden beads for the best results.

Belaying pins A model ship-building component available in wood in various sizes from model shops.

Brass pins Various sizes of brass pins are used in the projects, available from miniature hardware specialists.

Bunka This is perhaps better known as lampshade fringing and can be purchased either as fringing or tassels from haberdashery (notions) departments and fabric stores (see Basic Techniques, page 12, for tips on using bunka).

Centre cane Used in basket making and available from specialist outlets in various thicknesses. It is known as round reed cane in the USA.

Cocktail sticks A substitute for $1/16$in hardwood dowel. Fancy-ended cocktail sticks have a turned end and are available from Chinese supermarkets and craft stores.

Craft picks Flat wooden sticks with a rounded end, ideal for making handles.

Floral tape Normally used to bind stems of flowers and leaves together in cake decoration.

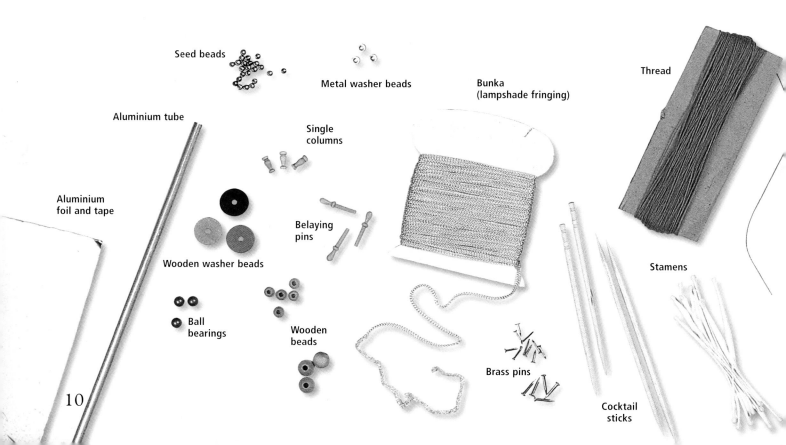

Seed beads

Metal washer beads

Bunka (lampshade fringing)

Thread

Aluminium tube

Single columns

Aluminium foil and tape

Belaying pins

Wooden washer beads

Stamens

Ball bearings

Wooden beads

Brass pins

Cocktail sticks

Jewellery findings Metal jewellery-making components, including head pins, eye pins and jump rings are used in many of the projects.

Paper ribbon A fine, creased paper normally used to make bows for floral arrangements.

Polymer clay Modelling clay that can be baked in domestic ovens to make designs solid and lasting. Various brands are available in many colours.

Quilling paper Narrow strips of paper, available in a range of colours and widths.

Single columns Model ship-building components, available in wood in various sizes from model shops.

Snap-fastener Also known as a press-stud.

Stamens These are arranged in the centre of a flower-head in cake decorating and are available in a range of sizes and colours

Tapestry canvas A needlework fabric with a mesh-like construction available in various gauges.

Threads Various threads are used in the projects. Carpet thread or linen thread may be used as an alternative to button thread.

Wire Jewellery-making wires or florist's stub wires are available in various gauges and either are suitable for the projects.

Safety tips

Be aware that all tools have sharp cutting edges and should be used and stored safely.

When sanding wood **always** wear a dust mask to prevent inhaling fine dust particles.

Ensure good ventilation when using oil- and wax-based products and resin-based adhesives.

Always wash your hands thoroughly at the end of each session.

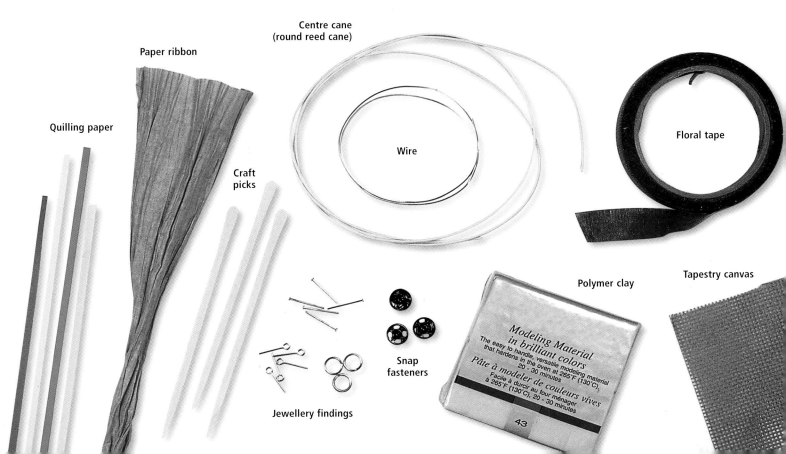

Quilling paper

Paper ribbon

Centre cane
(round reed cane)

Wire

Floral tape

Craft picks

Snap fasteners

Jewellery findings

Polymer clay

Tapestry canvas

Modeling Material in brilliant colors

43

Basic Techniques

This section covers the commonly used basic techniques required to make the projects and should be referred to when necessary.

Using Bunka

Bunka (fringing) will fray and curl if you pull a thread at the end of the braid and it is used to wig dolls and cover plastic animals. To keep the wavy effect frayed bunka should be laid, not pulled, on to the area of tacky glue it is covering. It can be laid any way as long as it is in an even layer. Don't touch the bunka until the glue has dried or it will be flattened.

Using Colouring Mediums

The projects use various colouring mediums, including water-based acrylic paints, oil-based enamel paints, shoe polish and wood stain.
- Apply paints with an artist's paintbrush: medium (approx. size 6) and fine (approx. size 000) are needed for the projects.
- Several of the projects use oil-based spray or enamel paints, follow the manufacturer's safety instructions when using these products. When painting on metal use a metal primer to provide a surface for the top coat to adhere to.
- Apply shoe polish to wood using fine-gauge wire wool and buff up to a sheen with clean wire wool or a cloth. Avoid using polish on edges to be glued, as the bond will not be as strong.
- Apply wood stain to wood, card and paper using a soft cloth and use sparingly as too much stain can warp wood. Stain parts before assembly, allowing them to dry completely.

Cutting Wood

Use a craft knife, mitre cutters or a saw to cut wood and cut so that the grain runs in line with the sides that have the longest measurement, unless otherwise stated. Sand and polish wood following the grain.

Chamfering means creating an angle at the edge of a piece of wood. The simplest method is to hold the piece of wood upright (at a slight angle) above fine-grade sandpaper, with the edge to be chamfered facing down. Sand the edge in small sweeping motions in the same direction, until you achieve the correct angle. Two angles, 45 and 75, are drawn here to help you.

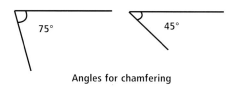

Angles for chamfering

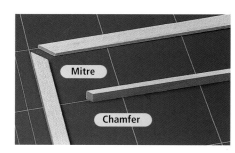

Mitring means cutting the ends of two wood pieces to angles of 45 degrees so that they can be fitted together to make a right-angled joint. Use a mitre block and saw for this, positioning the saw in the slits of the mitre block to cut diagonally through the wood. Mitre cutters should have the wood pressed against the guide to achieve a 45-degree cut.

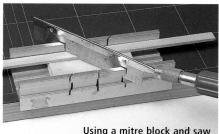

Using a mitre block and saw

Distressing Surfaces

This technique is used to imitate age and wear and tear to a surface. Wood in particular responds well to distressing treatments and two simple but effective methods are described here.
- To create a mature shine on wood to indicate continued polishing and handling, first apply brown shoe polish with fine-grade wire wool on to bare wood and then rub black shoe polish into some areas. Take a clean piece of wire wool and rub with the grain to create the patina of old age. Wood stain and shoe polish used sparingly are also excellent for achieving aged finishes on other materials.
- A wooden surface painted with water-based paints can be sanded in places where natural wear and tear would occur to reveal the bare wood. Use a paintbrush and cover the whole article with a light water-based stain such as antique pine or light oak. With a piece of damp cloth remove the stain from the wood in accessible areas. The stain will settle in the cracks and will colour the bare wood, creating the effect of worn paint and a build-up of grime.

Using Templates

Many of the projects have templates for you to use. Black and white templates are to be found on page 62 and colour templates on page 61.
- Black and white templates can simply be traced using a pencil and tracing paper.
- Colour templates should be reproduced either by colour photocopying on to white paper or card or by scanning the image into a computer and printing on photo-quality card or paper.

Toys That Teach

Building Blocks

Children have played with simple wooden bricks for centuries. Building blocks didn't become a commercially viable product until the 1880s, when boxes of architectural bricks began to be exported from Germany. The blocks were made out of cast cement and came in a variety of shapes, including arches and columns. Following their success, other factories in Europe began to produce similar sets made out of wood.

This project uses jelutong wood to make the bricks, as it is particularly suited to cutting into small, fine pieces. It can however, be substituted with other wood if desired.

You will need

$1/16$in thick obechi sheet wood:
  1in x $3/4$in for tray base
  two $1 1/8$in x $3/16$in for tray ends
  two $3/4$in x $3/16$in for tray sides

$1/8$in x $1/8$in jelutong wood:
  two $3/8$in lengths
  four $1/8$in lengths

$5/16$in x $1/8$in jelutong wood,
three $5/16$in lengths

$1/8$in x $1/16$in jelutong wood:
  four $3/8$in lengths
  four $1/4$in lengths
  six $1/8$in lengths

$1/8$in diameter hardwood dowel,
four $1/8$in lengths

Two 6mm single columns

Wood stain

Water-based acrylic paints

Tacky glue

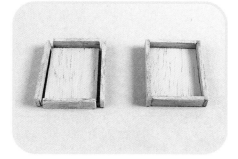

1 Sand each of the tray components using fine-grade sandpaper, stain and leave to dry. Once dry, glue the tray sides and ends on to the outside edges of the base, so that the base is sandwiched between.

2 Take the three pieces of $5/16$in x $1/8$in jelutong wood. Cut one piece corner to corner to form two triangles. Drill a hole centrally through each of the other pieces using $1/8$in drill bit, then cut to form an arch.

3 Sand the remaining wood pieces and colour them using watered-down acrylic paints. Once dry, arrange and glue the building blocks into the tray.

Variation

The buildings in this photograph are no higher than $1/4$in and have been made out of jelutong wood. Once cut to size the buildings can either be painted or left natural.
Large buildings – $3/16$in x $1/8$in strip wood with $1/8$in triangular strip wood.
Medium buildings – $1/8$in x $3/32$in strip wood with $3/32$in triangular strip wood.
Small buildings – $1/8$in x $1/16$in strip wood with $1/16$in triangular strip wood.

Abacus

Frames of beads used for counting and simple mathematical calculations date back to ancient times. Nowadays we assume that the abacus is just used to teach children to count, however it is still a very useful tool in many shops and offices in Eastern countries. Traditionally in Britain the abacus has rows of ten beads, however, wires with twelve or six beads were common during the period of the imperial measuring system.

You will need

$^3/_8$in x $^1/_8$in obechi strip wood, two 1in lengths

$^3/_{64}$in diameter hardwood dowel, two 1in lengths

24-gauge silver-coloured wire, five 1in lengths

Fifty cream seed beads, size 11

Wood stain

Tacky glue

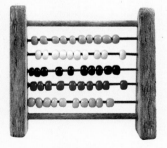

Variation

The abacus used in the main project uses cream seed beads to represent bone beads, for an abacus from the Victorian era and onwards use coloured seed beads, as shown here (shown larger than actual size).

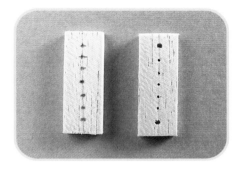

1 Take the two obechi wood pieces and make a pencil mark every $^1/_8$in centrally along the length of each. Use a $^3/_{64}$in drill bit to drill a hole halfway through the wood at the top and bottom marks. The five remaining marks should have a hole drilled halfway through the wood using a $^1/_{64}$in drill bit.

2 At one short end on each wood piece mark $^1/_8$in inwards from each corner. Draw a pencil line from the opposite corners up to the marks and cut along the lines with a craft knife.

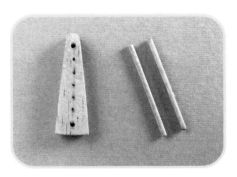

3 Sand and shape the narrow ends of each wood piece using fine-grade sandpaper and then stain them. Stain the two pieces of dowel as well.

4 Position and glue the two dowels and five lengths of wire into one wood piece. With the ends of the wires upwards, thread ten beads on to each. Secure by lining up the ends of the wire and dowel with the holes on the remaining wood piece and glue into position.

Xylophone

The xylophone originated in South-east Asia and arrived in Europe during the 16th century, however, it was not until the end of the 19th century that it was first played in an orchestra. Toy versions of the xylophone were, and still are, a popular choice of children's musical toys. The xylophone that we are making here is suitable for any nursery from the Victorian era onwards.

You will need

$^1/_{16}$in x $^1/_{16}$in thick obechi strip wood, two 1in lengths

2mm wide quilling paper in a selection of colours

Centre (reed) cane size 000, $1^1/_2$in length

Two silver seed beads, size 11

Silver gel pen

Tacky glue

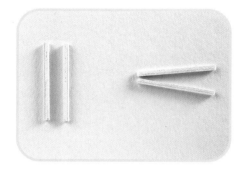

1 Sand the ends of the wood using fine-grade sandpaper. Run a small amount of glue along one side edge of each of the wood strips and position into a V shape, with the glued side upwards.

2 Cut eight $^3/_4$in lengths of quilling paper in eight different colours, place on top of the glued pieces of wood at regular intervals and leave to dry.

Variation

To make a xylophone with a metal-effect frame and beaters, paint the wood with silver acrylic paint before assembling and substitute the centre cane with 24-gauge florist's stub wire (xylophone shown larger than actual size).

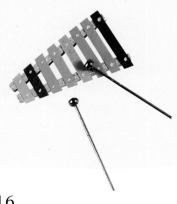

3 Turn the xylophone upside-down and trim the ends of the bars with sharp scissors. Use a silver gel pen to mark the bars with a dot at each end to give the effect of a nail head.

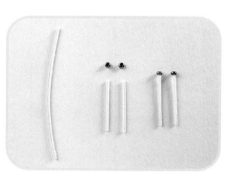

4 Soak the centre cane in warm water for a few minutes and then weigh down each end after pulling straight. Once dry, cut in half, so that you have two $^3/_4$in lengths. Glue a silver seed bead on the end of each piece of cane to make two beaters.

Picture Bricks

Building bricks covered with pictures were first made in the 1840s. Each brick was covered with different images, and could be put together in six different ways to create six different pictures. The Victorians were keen on the educational value of toys and this type of puzzle became particularly popular. Here we are creating the effect of a box of picture bricks.

You will need

³/₁₆in thick obechi sheet wood, ¹⁵/₁₆in x ¹⁵/₁₆in

¹/₄in x ¹/₁₆in obechi strip wood:
two 1¹/₁₆in lengths
two ¹⁵/₁₆in lengths

White card for colour photocopying

Light brown shoe polish

Tacky glue

Variation

Create a different picture bricks scene using an alternative painting – see colour templates on page 61, or use a favourite image of your own by reducing the size on a photocopier or scanner (picture bricks shown larger than actual size).

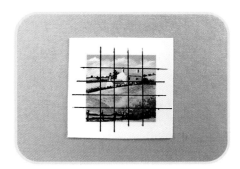

1 Colour photocopy one of the pictures (page 61) on to white card. Use a pencil and ruler to divide your picture into ³/₁₆in squares.

2 Use a craft knife and ruler to score over the pencil lines on the picture, taking care not to cut right through the card. Rub out any pencil lines still showing with a soft rubber and then cut out the picture.

3 Use fine-grade sandpaper to sand smooth any rough edges on the wooden components. Colour the wood strips and one side only of the wooden block with a brown shoe polish.
Position and glue the picture on to the unstained side of the wooden block. Once dry, rub over with a small amount of light brown shoe polish to age and accentuate the blocks (see Basic Techniques, page 12).

4 Place the short side wood pieces opposite each other and glue on to the outside edges of the wooden block. Position and glue the longer side pieces to the remaining outside edges of the base.

Blackboard

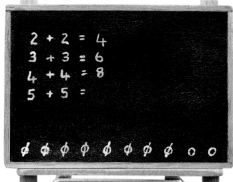

Children love to play at being grown-up and what better than being the 'teacher' in a game of schools. The blackboard has been the main teaching aid in a classroom situation for decades, although nowadays it seems to have largely been replaced by the whiteboard and the flip chart. This free-standing blackboard is set on an easel is thought to be suitable for nurseries from the Edwardian period (early 20th century) onwards.

You will need

$\frac{3}{16}$in x $\frac{1}{16}$in jelutong wood:
  two 3$\frac{1}{2}$in lengths for front legs
  three 2$\frac{1}{8}$in lengths for two long front supports and shelf
  two 1$\frac{3}{4}$in lengths for short front supports
  two 3$\frac{1}{4}$in lengths for back legs
  two 1$\frac{1}{2}$in lengths for back supports

$\frac{1}{16}$in thick bass sheet wood, 2$\frac{1}{4}$in x 1$\frac{5}{8}$in

$\frac{1}{16}$in x $\frac{1}{16}$in jelutong wood:
  two 2$\frac{3}{8}$in lengths
  two 1$\frac{5}{8}$in lengths

Small brass hinge

Button thread

Centre (reed) cane size 000, $\frac{1}{4}$in length

Acrylic water-based paints

Wood stain

Tacky glue and epoxy resin glue

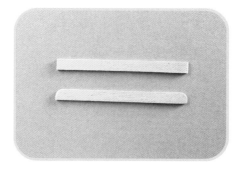

1 Take the shelf wood piece and use fine-grade sandpaper to round the corners on one long side.

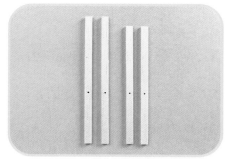

2 Take a front leg, and mark 1$\frac{3}{8}$in along from one end centrally. Drill a hole at this point through the wood using a $\frac{3}{64}$in drill bit. Repeat with the remaining front leg and the two back legs. Sand and stain all of the strip wood pieces. Sand and paint the sheet wood on each side with black acrylic paint.

3 Place the $\frac{1}{16}$in x $\frac{1}{16}$in strip wood pieces next to the corresponding side edges of the painted board and glue into place. Once dry, slightly round the corner using fine-grade sandpaper, touching up with stain.

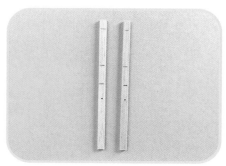

4 Take the front legs of the easel and from the top (drilled hole towards the bottom of the leg), measure and mark the following positions on each – $\frac{1}{4}$in, 1$\frac{1}{4}$in and 1$\frac{3}{4}$in.

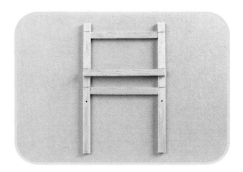

5 Place the legs 1³/₄in apart. Position two short front supports and one long front support as shown and glue into place. The top of the wood strips should be in line with the pencil marks.

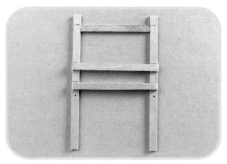

6 Position and glue the remaining front support on top of the support that is immediately above the drill holes.

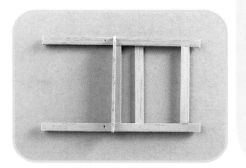

7 Turn the construction over and position and glue the shelf on to the front of the easel, with the underside of the shelf flush with the edge of the supports.

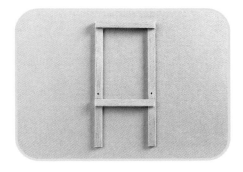

8 Take the back legs of the easel and from the top (drilled hole towards the bottom of the leg), measure and mark 2in down. Place the legs 1¹/₈in apart, position the back supports as shown and glue into place.

9 Attach the frames by positioning as shown and gluing a small brass hinge into place with epoxy resin glue.

10 Take a length of button thread and knot one end. Thread through the front of the easel to the back of the easel. Knot the opposite end so that there is approximately 1in of thread between the frames. Repeat the procedure on the other side.

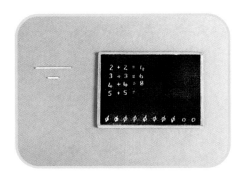

11 Make a piece of chalk from a short length of centre cane, painted with white acrylic paint. Write or draw on the blackboard using a fine paintbrush and white acrylic paint.

Variation

Make a small hand-held blackboard (shown here larger than actual size) from a 1in x ³/₄in piece of ¹/₁₆in thick bass sheet wood. Edge the board with two ³/₄in lengths of ¹/₁₆in x ¹/₁₆in jelutong strip wood and two 1¹/₈in lengths, following the instructions in step 3.

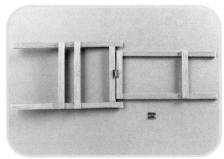

Hammer and Pegs

Wooden toys have been made since ancient times, when they were mainly miniature replicas of items used by adults in everyday life. During the Victorian years, Germany was considered to be the centre of the wooden toy-making industry, exporting all over Europe. This hammer and peg set would be suitable for any nursery from the Edwardian era and onwards.

You will need

$^1/_{16}$in thick bass sheet wood:
  $^7/_8$in x $^1/_2$in for pegboard
  two $^5/_8$in x $^1/_2$in for side supports

$^1/_8$in diameter hardwood dowel,
$^1/_4$in length for hammer head

$^3/_{64}$in diameter hardwood dowel,
$^3/_4$in length for hammer shaft

Two cocktail sticks

Wood stain

Acrylic water-based paints

Tacky glue

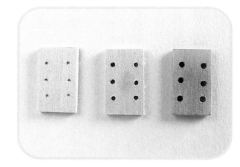

1 Transfer the hole positions from the pegboard template (page 62) on to the pegboard wood piece. Drill a series of holes through the wood, using a $^1/_{32}$in drill bit first, followed by a $^1/_{16}$in drill bit. Use fine-grade sandpaper to sand smooth and then colour the wood with a light wood stain.

2 Take a side support and measure halfway across the longest length and mark with a pencil. Make a groove by placing in a mitre block and sawing halfway through the wood on each side of the pencil line. Use a craft knife to carefully remove the wood between the two lines. Use fine-grade sandpaper to clean and sand smooth the section until it is wide enough to hold the $^1/_{16}$in thick pegboard. Repeat with the other side support and then paint each piece with acrylic paints.

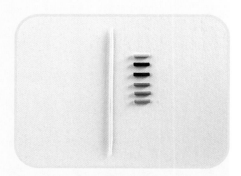

3 Make pegs from six $^3/_8$in lengths cut from a cocktail stick. Sand the ends and paint each peg with water-based acrylic paints.

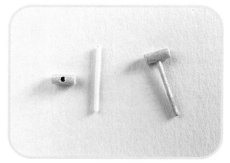

4 Take the hammer head piece and drill a hole centrally, drilling only part-way through the wood using a $^3/_{64}$in drill bit. Stain the hammer head and shaft to match the pegboard. Position and glue the hammer head on to the end of the shaft.

5 Position and glue the pegboard into the grooves in the side supports, leave to dry and then place the pegs into the pegboard, as shown in the finished picture.

Rattle

As might be imagined, rattles have a long history; as well as amusing a baby, the noise was thought to ward off evil spirits. The rattle made here is based upon a French *poupard* which was popular during the second half of the 19th century. A *poupard* often had some kind of musical movement concealed under its 'skirt' so that when the stick was swung slowly around the music began to play. Bells were often sewn on to the costume or the hat for extra effect.

You will need

Coloured paper

Paper ribbon in a contrasting colour

Natural round wooden bead, 4mm diameter

Fancy-ended cocktail stick

Thirteen metallic seed beads, size 14

Hair-coloured bunka (lampshade fringing), 1in length

Paper punches, regular sun, mini sun and $1/16$in circle

Acrylic water-based paints

Tacky glue

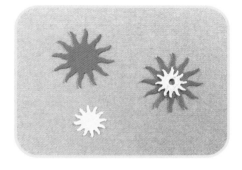

1 Make the cloak by punching a regular sun shape out of coloured paper and a mini sun out of paper ribbon. Place the mini sun on top of the regular sun and, using a needle or $1/16$in paper punch, make a hole through the centre of each. (If you don't have paper punches, trace and cut out the templates on page 62).

2 Cut the cocktail stick to $1/2$in. Thread the shapes on to the straight end of the stick (this may need to be shaved slightly using a craft knife) and fold. Allow $1/8$in of the cocktail stick to protrude and glue the wooden bead on to this.

3 Make the hat from a piece of paper ribbon $1/2$in x $3/8$in (creases running with longest length). Follow the stages as shown, gluing the flap down at stage 3. Position and glue the hat on the head and paint the features using acrylic paints and a fine paintbrush.

4 Run a line of glue around the brim of the hat and lay a length of frayed bunka on top for hair (see Basic Techniques, page 12). To finish, glue the seed beads on to the tips of the cloak and the point of the hat to give the effect of lots of bells!

Paper Toys

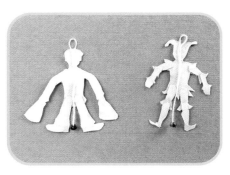

Advances in printing technology from the mid 19th century onwards meant that paper toys could be produced cheaply and easily. They were often sold in sheet form, to be coloured in and cut out. Here we create the effect of a jumping Jack. Traditionally, the movable limbs were held together with knotted string and made to move by pulling a long piece hanging behind the body.

Number cubes were used in various games of chance, although would not have been particularly durable if made from paper or card.

You will need

White paper for colour photocopying

Cream cotton thread, $2^1/2$in length

Two seed beads, size 14

Tacky glue

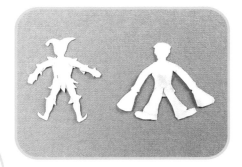

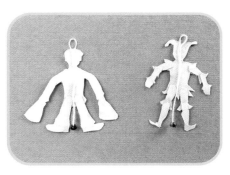

1 To make the jumping Jacks, colour photocopy the jumping Jacks on page 61 on to white paper. Cut out the bodies and limbs with small, sharp scissors. Glue the arms and legs on to the back of the body.

2 To enable the Jacks to be hung up, cut two $1^1/4$in lengths of cotton thread. Make a small loop at one end of each and glue on to the backs of the Jacks, with the loops immediately above the heads and the thread falling between the legs. Glue a seed bead on to the end of the thread to represent a bell pull.

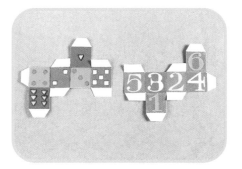

3 To make the number cubes, colour photocopy the cubes from page 61 on to white paper. Use a craft knife and metal ruler to lightly score along any inside lines. Cut out the templates with small, sharp scissors. Fold into shape, dabbing tiny amounts of glue on to the flaps to hold in place.

Push and Pull Toys

Rocking Horse

The first rocking horses were designed in Germany at the beginning of the 17th century – simple toys with semicircles of wood for sides, a block of wood for a seat and a carved head. Horses' legs were often painted on the sides and eventually a gap was cut between the legs. By the end of the 18th century the semicircles were replaced with bow-shaped rockers. This horse is based on early designs, its simplicity making it suitable for nurseries of the Stuart, Georgian and Regency eras and a more affordable toy for less wealthy Victorians and Edwardians.

You will need

$^3/_{32}$in thick bass sheet wood:
  two 3$^1/_2$in x 1$^1/_4$in for rockers
  1$^1/_4$in x 1in for head
  1$^1/_4$in x $^1/_2$in for seat
  $^5/_8$in x $^1/_2$in for front support
  1$^1/_4$in x $^1/_2$in for back-rest

Cocktail stick 1$^3/_8$in long for feet support

Two wooden belaying pins, 14mm long for handles

Wood stain or shoe polish

Tacky glue

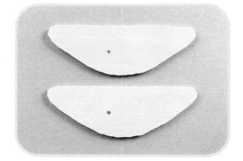

1 Transfer the rocker template (page 62) on to the two pieces of wood. Use mitre cutters to cut around the outline of the rockers. Shape and sand smooth the edges, using medium-grade sandpaper then fine-grade. Using a $^1/_{16}$in drill bit, drill a hole through each rocker, using the template for the position.

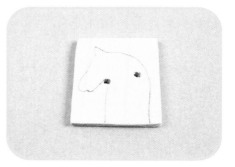

2 Transfer the horse's head template (page 62) on to the wood piece (grain running with head height). To avoid the wood splitting whilst being cut, drill a hole through the wood under the neck of the horse using a $^1/_{16}$in drill bit and begin cutting from here. Now drill a hole through the head as shown on the template.

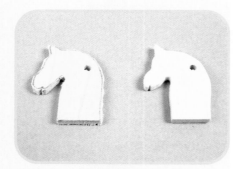

3 Use mitre cutters to cut around the outline of the horse's head, shaping and smoothing with sandpaper as before.

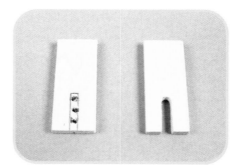

4 Transfer the seat template (page 62) on to the wood. Drill a series of $^1/_{16}$in holes, using the template as a guide. Clean out with a craft knife and sand using fine-grade sandpaper. Ensure the head slots into this opening. Widen with medium-grade sandpaper if necessary.

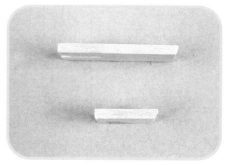

5 On the opposite end to the seat opening, chamfer the edge of the wood to an angle of 75 degrees (see page 12) using medium-grade sandpaper. Chamfer the edge of one of the short ends of the front support section to an angle of 75 degrees.

6 Take the back-rest piece of wood and round the corners at one short end using medium-grade sandpaper followed by fine-grade sandpaper.

7 Remove nearly all of the straight section of wood from the belaying pins using mitre cutters, leaving just less than $^1/_{16}$in attached to the turned head. Stain or shoe polish all wooden components and leave to dry.

8 Position and glue the head into the opening on the seat section, making sure that the chamfered edge at the opposite end is facing downwards.

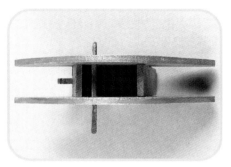

9 Place a rocker face down on a flat surface. Rest the side edge of the seat on top so that the top of the seat is flush with the straight edge of the rocker. The horse's head should be above the drilled hole in the rocker. Position the back-rest against the chamfered end of the seat, so that it lies at an angle with the shaped end about $^1/_2$in higher than the seat. Now re-position the seat and back-rest so that there is equal distance from the end of the rocker to the front of the seat, and from behind the back-rest to the other end of the rocker. Glue into place. The chamfered edge of the front support should sit immediately below the front of the seat and be glued into position.

10 Place the remaining rocker on top of the construction, with its drilled hole in line with the hole on the opposite rocker and glue into place. For the foot support, thread the cocktail stick through the rocker holes with an even amount protruding on each side. Dab a tiny amount of glue around the inside edge of the drilled holes to secure the foot support in place.

11 Position and glue the straight ends of the belaying pins into the hole on each side of the head. If you find that your rocking horse is not balanced, very carefully sand the base of the rockers using fine-grade sandpaper until it stands straight.

Variation

To make a painted rocking horse suitable for Victorian and Edwardian eras, follow the previous instructions, apart from staining. Paint your horse using water-based acrylics, referring to the barrel horse (page 27) for the facial features. The rocking horse shown here has a distressed finish to simulate old age (see Basic Techniques page 12). Make a saddle from a 1in x $^3/_4$in piece of fine leather. Fold the short edges underneath so that it measures $^3/_4$in x $^1/_2$in. Position and glue the folded leather piece on to the rocking horse seat.

Barrel Horse

Small log-shaped barrel horses on wheeled platforms originated in Germany during the 15th century. They began to be manufactured in Britain during the 18th century and became particularly popular during the Victorian and Edwardian eras, as unlike their expensive relative the rocking horse, they were more affordable to less wealthy children. The painted push-along barrel horse here is typical of the 19th and early 20th century.

You will need

$^3/_{32}$in thick bass sheet wood, 1$^1/_4$in x 1$^1/_4$in for head

$^1/_2$in diameter hardwood dowel, 1$^1/_4$in length for body

$^1/_2$in x $^1/_8$in bass strip wood, 1$^1/_4$in length for trolley

Six craft picks for legs and handle

Cocktail stick for handle

Four 10mm wooden washer beads

Four $^1/_4$in long brass pins

Fine glove leather, 1$^1/_8$in x $^1/_2$in

Water-based acrylic paints

1 Transfer the barrel horse's head template (page 62) on to the wood, with the wood grain running with the height of the head. To avoid the wood splitting whilst being cut, drill a hole through the wood under the neck using a $^1/_{16}$in drill bit and begin cutting from here.

2 Use mitre cutters to cut around the outline of the head, then use medium-grade sandpaper, followed by fine-grade sandpaper to shape and sand smooth any rough edges.

3 Using a craft knife, shave off a small section from the curved part of the wood dowel to form a flat area the length of the dowel and $^3/_8$in wide. Sand smooth.

4 Refer to the barrel horse trolley and body template (page 62) and transfer the drill hole positions on to the flat side of the dowel. Using a $^1/_{16}$in drill bit, drill holes about $^1/_8$in deep (for the legs later).

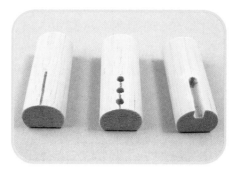

5 On the dowel's curved side, make a pencil mark $^1/_2$in long at one end. Using a $^1/_{16}$in bit, drill holes along the line, $^1/_8$in deep. Use a craft knife and medium-grade sandpaper to clean the drilled section. This groove should be long and deep enough to secure the head later.

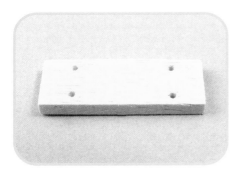

6 Using the trolley and body template (page 62), transfer the drill hole positions on to the trolley. Using a ³⁄₆₄in bit, drill holes which will eventually secure the legs into place. Do not drill all the way through the wood.

7 Measure and mark ¹⁄₈in along on the longest outside edges of the trolley, at each end and on both sides. Using a ¹⁄₃₂in drill bit, drill a hole at each point so that the wheels can be pinned into place later.

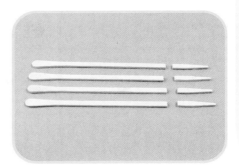

8 The legs are made with the pointed ends from four craft picks, cut to ³⁄₄in long. The widest end of each of the legs should fit into the holes on the underside of the body. If not, shave slightly so that they can be fitted later.

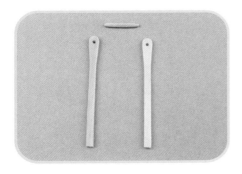

9 The handle is made with the rounded ends from two craft picks, cut to 2in long. Use a ³⁄₆₄in drill bit to drill a hole through the rounded end of each pick. Cut a cocktail stick to measure ⁵⁄₈in long and gently taper each end using fine-grade sandpaper so that each end can be inserted into the craft picks later.

10 Glue the head into the groove on the body. Glue the widest end of the legs into the holes on the underside of the body. The width of the legs should run along the length of the body. Dab glue on to the feet and secure into the holes on top of the trolley. Once dry, paint with water-based acrylic paints.

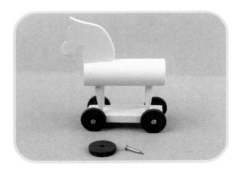

11 Paint the wooden washer beads and handle components to match or contrast with previous painting.

For the wheels, thread a brass pin into a wooden washer, dab a spot of glue on to the pin end and secure into a hole on the base side. Allow the wheel to turn by not pressing too hard into position. Repeat for the other wheels.

12 Transfer the saddle template (page 62) on to the underside of the fine glove leather. Cut out using sharp scissors then glue on to the horse. Next, refer to the photograph, left, and paint the facial features on to both sides of the head with a fine paintbrush.

13 Taking the handle components, insert and glue each end of the cocktail stick into the hole in each craft pick. Glue the bottom of the handle on to the sides of the trolley, just in front of the back wheels and angled towards the back of the horse.

Variation

To create the effect of a pre-Victorian barrel horse, instead of painting it, stain or shoe polish each of the individual wooden components. Leave to dry before assembling.

27

Sheep on Wheels

Margaret Steiff designed the first commercial soft-bodied pull-along toys in Germany in 1886. Early Steiff sheep were made from real lamb's wool and stuffed with left-over pieces of leather. In 1895 her toys were first exported to Britain, and the pull-along sheep on wheels proved to be particularly popular. Steiff's other farm animals on wheels included horses, donkeys, pigs and goats.

You will need

Plastic toy sheep no more than 1in high

Cream bunka (lampshade fringing) about 60in length

Black polymer clay

$^3/_{32}$in thick obechi sheet wood, $1^1/_4$in x $^5/_8$in for trolley

Four 7mm top sections from black snap-fasteners

Four $^3/_8$in long fine brass pins or gold-plated head pins

One $^1/_2$in gold-plated head pin

Button thread, 4in length

Tacky glue

Wood stain or shoe polish

Old gold-coloured spray paint or gold metallic paste

Epoxy resin glue

1 Start by fraying the bunka (see page 12). Apply a thin even layer of tacky glue over the back legs. Lay the bunka on a hoof and start to cover the leg, winding and laying the bunka around and up the leg so it is evenly covered. Once at the top, work down the other back leg, keeping the bunka neat and even.

2 Apply tacky glue over the back end of the sheep. Manoeuvre the bunka so that it covers the bottom area and then begin to wind and lay it around the body. Leave to dry before covering the front legs and head, otherwise the bunka will be pressed into the glue and your sheep will end up with a matted woollen coat!

3 Apply tacky glue over the front legs and head and continue to cover with the frayed bunka.

4 Make two eyes and a nose by rolling out three tiny balls of black polymer clay. Harden by baking in a domestic oven, following the instructions on the packet. Once baked and cool glue the eyes and nose into place.

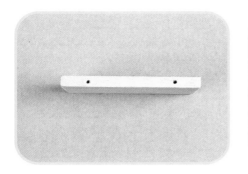

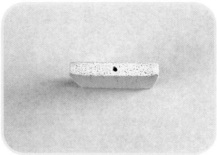

5 Sand the edges of the trolley piece using fine-grade sandpaper. Mark $^1/_4$in along on the longest outside edges, at each end and on both sides. Drill a $^1/_{32}$in hole at each point for the wheels later.

6 Measure and mark half-way across one of the shortest outside edges and using a $^1/_{32}$in drill bit, drill a hole at this point, for the towing pin later. Use wood stain or shoe polish to colour the trolley.

7 The snap-fasteners are used as wheels and should either be sprayed with an old gold-coloured spray paint or rubbed over with a gold metallic paste to give an aged effect.

8 To attach the wheels to the trolley, thread a $^3/_8$in brass pin or head pin in through the hole on the patterned side of a snap-fastener. Dab a tiny amount of tacky glue on the end of the pin and secure into one of the holes on the side edge of the base. Allow for wheel movement by not pressing too hard into position. Repeat for the other three wheels.

9 To make a towing pin, bend the $^1/_2$in head pin into an L shape, dab a spot of tacky glue on the straight end and secure upright into the hole on the front edge of the trolley. Make a loop at one end of the button thread, hook on to the pin and pull tight. Rather than knot the thread, which will look bulky, dab a tiny amount of glue where the threads meet. Once dry, trim excess with sharp scissors.

To finish, position the sheep on the trolley and fix using epoxy resin glue on the hooves.

Variation Other plastic toy farm animals can be covered using the same method, altering the size of the trolley and snap-fastener wheels depending on the size of the animal.

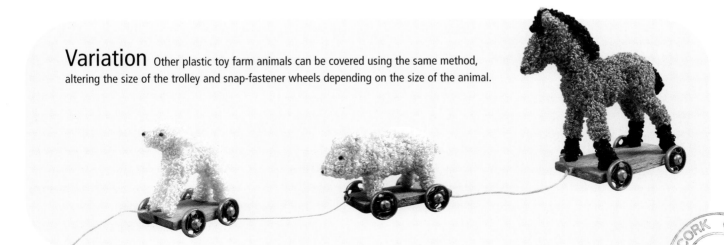

Train Set

The production of toy trains did not begin until the 1830s and were made very simply out of wood. As the century progressed, so did the production and quality of the toy train, and by the beginning of the 20th century mechanical train sets made out of tin plate became every boy's dream. The simple wooden train set described here is suitable for any nursery from the beginning of the Victorian era onwards.

You will need

For the engine:

$^1/_4$in x $^1/_{16}$in obechi strip wood, $^1/_2$in length for base

$^1/_8$in x $^1/_8$in obechi strip wood, $^1/_4$in length for cabin

$^1/_{32}$in thick obechi sheet wood, $^3/_{16}$in x $^3/_{16}$in for cabin roof

$^1/_8$in diameter hardwood dowel, $^1/_4$in length for engine

Cocktail stick $^3/_{16}$in long for funnel

Four 3mm metal washer beads

Four $^5/_{32}$in long brass pins or gold-plated head pins

Gold-plated eye pin

Tacky glue

Wood stain

For the carriages:

$^1/_4$in x $^1/_{16}$in obechi strip wood, two $^1/_2$in lengths for base

$^1/_8$in x $^1/_8$in obechi strip wood, two $^3/_8$in lengths for freight

Eight 3mm metal washer beads

Eight $^5/_{32}$in long brass pins or gold-plated head pins

Three gold-plated eye pins

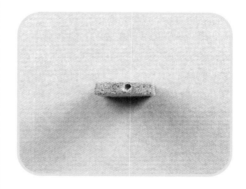

1 Begin by sanding each of the individual wooden components using fine-grade sandpaper and then stain.

2 Measure $^1/_8$in along on the longest outside edges of the engine base, at each end and on both sides. Using a $^1/_{64}$in drill bit, drill a hole at each point for the wheels later. Repeat this with the two carriage bases.

3 To enable the engine and carriages to hook together later, measure half-way across one of the shortest outside edges on the engine base, and using a $^1/_{64}$in drill bit drill a hole at this point. Repeat this at one end of a carriage base. The remaining carriage base should have a hole drilled at each end as it will be the central carriage.

4 To attach the wheels to the engine base, thread a brass pin into a metal washer bead, dab a tiny amount of tacky glue on to the end of the pin and secure into one of the holes on the side edge of the base. Continue until the engine has four wheels. Repeat this with the carriage bases.

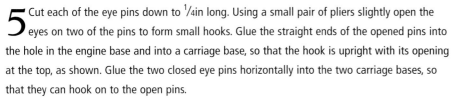

5 Cut each of the eye pins down to ¹⁄₄in long. Using a small pair of pliers slightly open the eyes on two of the pins to form small hooks. Glue the straight ends of the opened pins into the hole in the engine base and into a carriage base, so that the hook is upright with its opening at the top, as shown. Glue the two closed eye pins horizontally into the two carriage bases, so that they can hook on to the open pins.

6 Take the dowel engine and mark ³⁄₃₂in from one end. Using a ¹⁄₃₂in drill bit, drill a small hole deep enough to take the point of the cocktail stick funnel. Glue the point of the cocktail stick into the engine.

7 Position the cabin, engine and roof on to the engine base as shown, gluing them into place.

8 Position and glue the freight pieces on to each of the carriage bases as shown. Finally, link the engine and carriages together by using the eye pins.

Doll's Pram

Prams began to be manufactured during the early Victorian era and many dolls' prams were smaller versions of full-sized models. A doll's pram known as a 'mailcart' was available during the 19th century – shaped rather like a push-chair, with a well for the doll's feet, iron wheels and handles. This deep-bodied doll's pram is based upon designs popular during the 1920s. The well has space for the doll's feet or could be covered with a lid and used to store bedding.

You will need

$^1/_{16}$in thick obechi sheet wood:
  two $1^3/_4$in x $1^5/_8$in for pram sides
  two $1^3/_4$in x $^{13}/_{16}$in for pram base
  and inside base
  $^{15}/_{16}$in x $^7/_8$in for pram front
  $1^7/_{16}$in x $^{15}/_{16}$in for pram back
  (grain to run with shortest length)
  $^{15}/_{16}$in x $^7/_8$in for hood back
  $^{15}/_{16}$in x $^9/_{16}$in for hood top

$^1/_{16}$in x $^1/_{16}$in obechi strip wood:
  two long ledge lengths $1^3/_4$in
  two short ledge lengths $^{13}/_{16}$in

Two craft picks for handle

Three cocktail sticks for handle and axle

Four 10mm wooden washer beads

$^1/_8$in diameter aluminium tube, two $^{13}/_{16}$in lengths

Metal primer

Tacky glue

Water-based acrylic paints

1 Take the pram back piece and chamfer the edge of one short side to an angle of 45 degrees using fine-grade sandpaper (see Basic Techniques page 12). Take the hood back piece and chamfer the edge of one of its long sides in the same way.

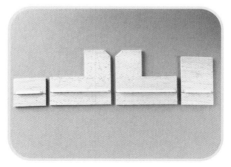

2 Transfer the pram side template (page 62) on to the two pieces of obechi wood. Using a craft knife and ruler cut out the shapes.

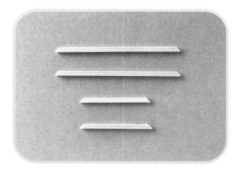

3 Take the four obechi strip ledge sections (which make a ledge for the inside base) and mitre the ends on each piece of wood to 45 degrees.

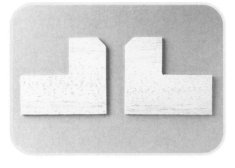

4 Place the pram front, sides and back (with top chamfer facing down) as shown. Transfer the ledge measurements from page 62 on to each piece. Glue the four ledges on to the pencil lines with mitred ends outwards.

5 Apply tacky glue to the longest outside edges of the base. Position the two sides beside the base (ledges facing). Glue the front and back on each end of the base, with mitred ends fitting together on the inside.

6 Transfer the inside base template (page 62) on to the inside base piece of wood. Cut where indicated and drill a hole through the middle section using a $^3/_{64}$in drill bit.

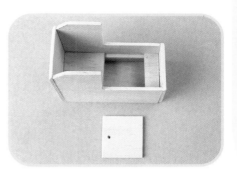

7 Glue two of the inside base pieces on to the ledge, leaving the piece with the drilled hole aside for the moment.

8 Place the hood back piece into position, so that the chamfered side edge of the hood back is at the top of the pram and is facing downwards. Place the hood top on top, neatly against the chamfered side edge of the hood back. Glue the hood pieces into place.

9 Shape the hood, rounding off the joined sections by sanding with medium-grade sandpaper then fine-grade.

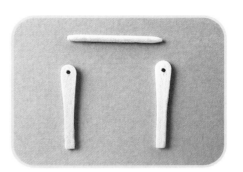

10 Make the handle from the rounded end of two craft picks, cut to 1in long. Using a $^3/_{64}$in drill bit, drill a hole through the rounded end of each pick. Cut a cocktail stick to $1^1/_{16}$in and taper the ends by sanding – to fit into the holes of the craft picks later. Cut the remaining two cocktail sticks to $1^3/_{16}$in long – for wheel axles later.

11 Paint the outside of the two pieces of aluminium tube with metal primer and leave to dry. Measure and mark $^1/_2$in from each end on the underside of the pram and use tacky glue to glue the two lengths of aluminium tube into place as shown. Leave to dry.

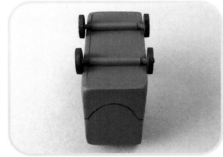

12 Paint the pram and handle components, wheels, axles and inside lid, with acrylic paints. Paint the detail on the outside of the pram by transferring the design from page 62 on to thin card. Cut along the outline. Place the card on to the sides of the pram and draw a pencil line along the edge, ensuring that the pattern meets at the corners. Paint the line.

13 Thread and glue a washer on to one end of a cocktail stick axle. Thread the axle through the aluminium tube and glue a wheel on to the opposite end. Repeat with the remaining axle. Taking the handle components, insert and glue each end of the cocktail stick into each of the craft pick holes. Referring to the main photograph, position and glue the bottom of the handle on to the sides of the pram so that it lies at a slight angle. Place the lid on to the ledge inside the pram.

Brick Truck

Crude versions of pull-along and push-along toys can be dated from times BC. Serving as an aid to walking as well as being a constructional toy, this push-along brick truck is suitable for any nursery from the Victorian era onwards. The solid wood building bricks have amused young children for many hours, giving them as much pleasure from building them up as knocking them down.

You will need

$^3/_{32}$in thick obechi sheet wood, 1$^1/_4$in x 1in for base

$^1/_{16}$in thick obechi sheet wood:
  two long sides 1$^3/_8$in x $^3/_8$in
  two short sides 1in x $^3/_8$in

$^3/_{16}$in x $^3/_{16}$in obechi strip wood, twelve $^3/_{16}$in lengths for bricks

Four 10mm wooden washer beads

Four $^1/_4$in long brass pins

Two craft picks for handle

Cocktail stick for handle

Tacky glue

Wood stain

Variation
Make a pull-along brick truck by substituting the handle for a towing pin. Refer to the sheep on wheels (page 28) for details of materials and instructions. To complete the project, glue a 4mm wooden bead on to the end of the rope.

1 Make the handle from the rounded ends of two craft picks, cut to 2in long. Use a $^3/_{64}$in drill bit to drill a hole through the rounded end of each pick. Cut a cocktail stick to 1$^1/_4$in long and taper each end using fine-grade sandpaper, so that they can be inserted into the craft picks later.

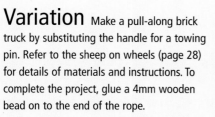

3 On the longest sides, measure $^1/_8$in along and $^1/_{16}$in up from the base at each end and on both sides. Using a $^1/_{32}$in drill bit, drill a hole at each point.

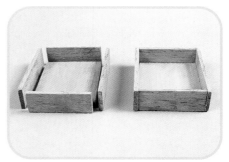

2 Use fine-grade sandpaper to sand smooth any rough edges on all the wooden components and then stain. Glue the short and long truck sides on to the outside edges of the base so that the base is sandwiched between, as shown.

4 Make the wheels by referring to page 27, step 11 (2nd paragraph). Make the handle by referring to page 27, step 13. Glue the bottom of the handle to the truck as shown in the main photograph above.

Dolls and Puppets

Toy Theatre

During the Victorian and Edwardian periods, a trip to the theatre would often have been re-created at home using a toy theatre. The theatres, usually made out of wood with paper scenery, had paper characters that were either mounted on wood or attached to wire so that they could be moved around the stage. Sheets with cut-out scenery and figures could be purchased either coloured or in black and white to be coloured at home. The theatre here is based upon a French toy theatre *circa* 1875.

You will need

$^1/_{16}$in thick obechi sheet wood:
  two 1$^3/_{16}$in x 1$^1/_8$in for sides
  1$^1/_4$in x 1$^1/_8$in for back
  1$^1/_2$in x $^7/_8$in for front arch

$^1/_8$in x $^1/_{16}$in obechi strip wood:
  1$^1/_2$in length
  two 1$^1/_8$in lengths

$^1/_8$in thick obechi sheet wood,
1$^1/_4$in x 1$^1/_8$in for base

$^3/_{64}$in diameter hardwood dowel,
three 1$^1/_2$in lengths

34-gauge jewellery wire,
4$^1/_2$in length

White paper for colour photocopying

Wood stain

Tacky glue

1 Take the front arch wood piece and mark $^1/_8$in along from each of the corners. Join the marks and then remove the corner sections using either mitre cutters or a craft knife. Round off two of the cuts on one long side of the wood using fine-grade sandpaper.

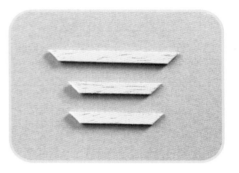

2 Take the three pieces of obechi strip wood and mitre the ends of each to an angle of 45 degrees (see Basic Techniques page 12). Stain the pieces sparingly, together with the front arch.

3 Make the theatre front by positioning and gluing the mitred wood strips and frontal arch together as shown.

4 Using white paper, colour photocopy the seven pieces of the toy theatre on page 61. Cut out the theatre front and top using small sharp scissors.

5 Glue the stage front cut-out on to the wooden theatre front, followed by the top cut-out – the scallops on this should slightly overlap the stage front cut-out.

6 Take the two side wood pieces and place them together. On the edges of one of the longest sides mark $^3/_8$in from one end, followed by $^1/_4$in and a further $^1/_4$in. Using a rounded pin file or fine-grade sandpaper folded in half, make grooves in the wood pieces at the marked points. The grooves should be wide and deep enough to hold $^3/_{64}$in diameter dowel. Sand and stain the remaining wooden components.

7 Cut out the castle backdrop and glue it on to the back wood piece, with the picture flush with the top of the wood and with an $^1/_8$in gap below the backdrop. Now position and glue the back and side wood pieces on to the outside edges of the base, positioning the $^3/_8$in grooves at the back of the theatre.

8 Position and glue the theatre front on to the front edges of the stage box, with the front protruding the sides by $^1/_{16}$in.

9 Cut out the three scenes and glue the top of each one centrally on to the lengths of dowel.

10 Drop the scenery on to the stage, so that the lengths of dowel rest in the slots at either side.

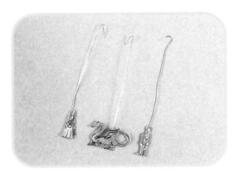

11 Cut out the figures and glue a $1^1/_2$in length of wire to the back of each. Bend the opposite end of the wire over to make a handle.

Puppet Theatre and Puppets

Originally, puppets were used to re-enact myths and legends, often with religious significance, and in some Far Eastern countries are still used for this purpose. Traditional to Europe are the glove puppets, Punch and Judy, who have entertained all classes of children for many years. Children would have played with this simple free-standing puppet theatre from the middle of the Victorian era onwards.

You will need

$1/16$in thick obechi sheet wood:
  two $4^5/8$in x $1^1/4$in for sides
  3in x 2in for front
  2in x $3/4$in for front arch
  2in x $1^1/4$in for top

$1/8$in x $1/16$in obechi strip wood,
2in length for shelf

$1/8$in x $1/8$in obechi strip wood:
  four $4^3/4$in lengths for legs

$3/64$in diameter hardwood dowel:
  $1^7/8$in length for front curtain pole
  two 1in lengths for puppets
  $3/4$in length for Punch's stick

Water-based acrylic paints

Paper punches, mini star and $5/8$in,
$1/4$in and $1/8$in diameter circles

Coloured paper

Paper ribbon

Cocktail stick

Skin-coloured polymer clay

Hair-coloured bunka (lampshade fringing)

Two medium, round flower stamens

Water-based wood stain

Tacky glue

1 Take the front arch piece of wood and mark $1/8$in along from the corners on one long side. Join the marks, then remove the two corners using either mitre cutters or a craft knife. Round off using fine-grade sandpaper.

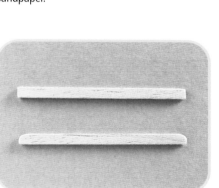

2 Take the shelf piece of wood and using fine-grade sandpaper, round the corners on one long side. Sand the remaining wooden components.

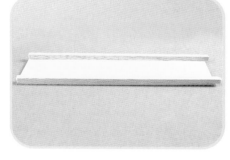

3 Take a side wood piece and two legs and glue the legs on to the side so that all edges are flush with each other, except for one end short end where $1/8$in of each leg should protrude. Repeat the procedure with the remaining side wood piece and legs.

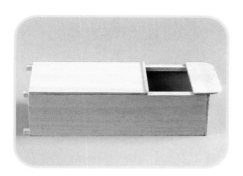

4 Position the side sections as shown and glue the front into place with all edges flush. Leave a gap of 1$\frac{1}{4}$in and glue the front arch in place, followed by the top and shelf. Once dry, paint the theatre with water-based acrylic paint. Punch paper shapes out of coloured paper and glue on to the front to decorate. Cover the shapes with a wash of light-coloured wood stain to age and add character (see distressing, page 12).

5 Paint the curtain pole to match the theatre. Make the curtains from two 1$\frac{3}{4}$in x $\frac{1}{4}$in lengths of paper ribbon (creases with longest length). Wind and glue the top of each piece around the dowel ends. Glue inside the theatre.

6 Make the back curtain from 3in x 1$\frac{7}{8}$in paper ribbon (creases to run with the longest length). Glue and wind the top around a 1$\frac{7}{8}$in long cocktail stick. Glue the covered pole on to the back of the theatre.

7 Punch and Judy's heads are made out of polymer clay. Roll a $\frac{5}{16}$in diameter ball for Punch and a $\frac{1}{4}$in ball for Judy. Press the end of a 1in length of dowel into each ball and very simply shape the heads. Harden by baking in a domestic oven (with dowel in place), following the manufacturer's instructions.

8 Refer to the main photograph and paint the facial features using water-based acrylic paints and a fine paintbrush. Make Punch's body following the instructions for the Jack-in-the-box on page 41, except that the paper creases should run vertically. Make Judy from two $\frac{5}{8}$in squares of paper ribbon in the same way. Punch $\frac{1}{8}$in circles out of paper ribbon to decorate their clothes and then glue together the sides of their gowns. (To age the puppets, cover the paper ribbon with a light wood stain and leave to dry before making up.)

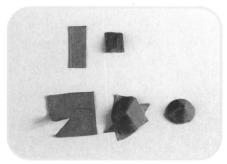

9 Make punch's hat from a $\frac{3}{4}$in x $\frac{1}{2}$in piece of paper ribbon, folded and glued in half lengthways. Shape and glue the back of the hat as shown and glue on to the head. Glue a small length of frayed bunka on to Punch's forehead. Make Judy's hat from a $\frac{3}{4}$in square of paper ribbon, forming the hat by cutting and gluing as shown. Run glue along her hairline and lay pieces of frayed bunka for hair, then glue her hat into place.

10 Complete the characters by staining a $\frac{3}{4}$in length of dowel for Punch and a $\frac{1}{2}$in length of cocktail stick for Judy and glue into place as shown.

Jack-in-the-Box

Jack-in-the-boxes originated during the 16th century. It is thought that the toy began as a practical joke, to shock a person unlatching the lid with a grotesque face springing up before them. Charles Dickens mentions in his book *The Cricket on the Hearth* (published in 1846) Tackleton the toy merchant, with his 'hideous, hairy, red-eyed Jack-in-the-boxes'. Here we are creating the effect of a more cheerful Jack-in-the-box that has just sprung out of his box!

You will need

$^{1}/_{32}$in thick card, 2in x 1in

Natural round wooden bead, 6mm diameter

Medium round flower stamen

Hair-coloured bunka (lampshade fringing) about 4in long

Paper ribbon in two contrasting colours

Cocktail stick, $^{7}/_{8}$in long

Gold-plated head pin

Gold-plated eye pin

Brown shoe polish

Gold metallic paste

Paper punch, mini sun

Tacky glue

Water-based acrylic paints

1 Transfer the Jack-in-the-box template (page 62) on to the card. Score along the inside lines using a craft knife and metal ruler – taking care not to cut right through the card!

2 Form a box by folding the card into shape as shown, with the scored lines on the outside of the box. At this stage the box will have a lid but no base. Secure the two edges of card that meet with tacky glue.

3 Insert the base into the box, trimming if necessary to ensure a good fit, and glue into position.

4 Paint the box with water-based acrylic paints. Once dry, age and add character by lightly rubbing over the surface with brown shoe polish and gold metallic paste.

5 Use the point of a small safety pin or a ¹/₆₄in drill bit to make a hole through the front of the box, as shown. Make a pencil mark ¹/₄in along the top edge of the lid and make another small opening in the card.

6 To make a catch for the box, cut the head off the head pin so that it measures ¹/₈in and glue the straight end into the hole in the front of the box. Cut the eye off the eye pin so it measures ¹/₄in. Hold the eye with a pair of pliers and bend to make an L shape. Glue the straight end of the eye pin into the opening on the edge of the lid.

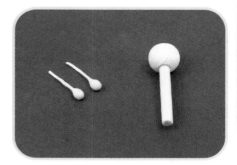

7 Thread and glue the wooden bead on to the end of the ⁷/₈in long cocktail stick so that the top of the bead is flush with the top of the stick. Make the arms with the flower stamen, the ends being the hands. Paint with a peach water-based acrylic paint. Once dry cut to ³/₈in long.

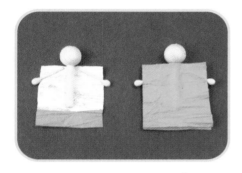

8 Cut two pieces of paper ribbon ³/₄in square in the same colour. Place on a flat surface, with the creases running horizontally. Spread a thin even layer of tacky glue over the top two-thirds on one side of each piece of paper ribbon. Position the cocktail stick and the stamen arms on the paper as shown. Place the other square of paper ribbon on top, like a sandwich, and leave to dry.

9 Cut the sandwiched section into shape with sharp scissors, as shown. Referring to circular photo detail below, paint the facial features on to the bead using water-based acrylic paints and a very fine paintbrush.

10 Cut out a mini sun shape with a paper punch (or by hand) from contrasting coloured paper ribbon. Cut out the centre to form a collar shape and glue around the front of Jack's neck. Make tiny cuffs to match, ¹/₁₆in wide x ¹/₄in long, gluing a strip around each wrist and trimming excess.

11 Make the wig by fraying a length of hair-coloured bunka (see Basic Techniques page 12). Apply a thin layer of tacky glue over the top of the head. Lay the frayed bunka along the hairline first and then cover the top of the head.

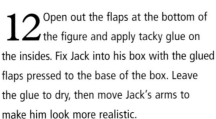

12 Open out the flaps at the bottom of the figure and apply tacky glue on the insides. Fix Jack into his box with the glued flaps pressed to the base of the box. Leave the glue to dry, then move Jack's arms to make him look more realistic.

Doll

Originally, dolls would not have been play things but a form of sacrificial offering or good luck charm. By the Middle Ages children began to play with dolls made out of wood or clay. During the 18th century doll's heads were wood or moulded papier mâché. Bisque (unglazed ceramic) heads were made in France and Germany from 1860, becoming popular during the late Victorian and Edwardian eras. Movable limbs, glass eyes and wigs became common features by the 20th century.

You will need

Paper ribbon in two contrasting colours

Natural round wooden bead 6mm diameter

Cocktail stick, $^1/_2$in long

Two medium round flower stamens

Hair-coloured bunka (lampshade fringing), 6in length

Tacky glue

Water-based acrylic paints

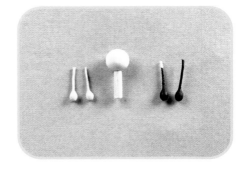

1 Glue the bead on to the end of the $^1/_2$in long cocktail stick, flush with the top of the stick. The ends of a stamen form the hands – paint them with peach acrylic paint. Once dry cut to $^3/_8$in long. The ends of another stamen form the shoes – paint and cut to $^1/_2$in long.

2 Cut two pieces of paper ribbon $^5/_8$in square in the same colour (creases running vertically). Spread tacky glue over one side of each piece. Place the cocktail stick, arms and legs on top of one piece as shown. Place the other square of paper ribbon on top. Leave to dry.

3 Cut the sandwiched section of paper ribbon into shape with scissors. Paint the facial features using water-based acrylic paints and a fine paintbrush.

4 Using the contrasting coloured paper ribbon, cut two tiny triangles and glue them on the dress as a collar. Make tiny cuffs $^1/_{16}$in x $^1/_4$in long to match, gluing a strip around each wrist. Make false pockets from two strips $^1/_{32}$in x $^1/_8$in, glued to the dress front.

5 The hair is made from frayed bunka (see Basic Techniques page 12). Apply a thin layer of tacky glue over the top of the head and lay the bunka from side to side so the hair rests on the shoulders and back. Once dry, trim untidy ends with scissors.

Variation

To make a clown doll, follow the same instructions but at step 3 cut out an upside-down V-shape from between the clown's legs. Paint the face and wig him (see page 41).

Parlour Games

Table-top Skittles

The game of table-top skittles dates back to ancient times. This indoor version was invented during the 18th century and became known as 'devil among the tailors'. In 1783 a group of tailors rioted after a production at the Theatre Royal in Haymarket, London, because they thought the play had insulted their profession. Soldiers intervened and reportedly brought the riot under control by using a technique like a ball crashing through a group of skittles.

You will need

$\frac{1}{16}$in thick obechi sheet wood:
  2in x 1$\frac{1}{8}$in for base
  $\frac{1}{2}$in x $\frac{1}{2}$in for platform

$\frac{1}{8}$in x $\frac{1}{16}$in obechi strip wood:
  two 2$\frac{1}{8}$in for long sides
  two 1$\frac{1}{8}$in for short sides

$\frac{1}{8}$in diameter hardwood dowel, 1$\frac{3}{4}$in length

Thin green card, 2in x 1$\frac{1}{8}$in

Fine chain, 1$\frac{3}{8}$in length

Two gold-plated eye pins

Cocktail stick

Natural round wooden bead 4mm diameter

Nine 6mm wooden single columns

Paper punch, $\frac{1}{8}$in diameter circle

Wood stain

Tacky glue

1 Transfer the hole position from the template on page 62 on to the wood base and the green card. Drill a hole through the wood using a $\frac{1}{8}$in drill bit and punch a $\frac{1}{8}$in hole out of the card. Glue the card on the base. Sand and stain all wooden components, including the base underside and leave to dry.

2 Glue the four sides of wood on to the outside edges of the base, so that the base is sandwiched between as shown. Glue the nine single columns on to the platform wood piece, and then position and glue on to the base.

3 Use a $\frac{1}{64}$in drill bit to drill a hole centrally into one end of the dowel. Cut an eye pin to measure $\frac{1}{2}$in, bend it into an L shape and glue the straight end into the dowel. Attach one end of the chain to the eye.

4 Fill the hole in the wooden bead with a cocktail stick, sanding to form a ball. Drill a $\frac{1}{64}$in hole in the ball and glue in the straight end of an eye pin cut to $\frac{1}{4}$in long. Attach the ball to the chain and slot the pole into the base.

Table-top Quoits

This table-top version of quoits, where rings are thrown at a peg with the aim of encircling it to score points, is related to the early pub game of throwing horseshoes at a pin in the ground. Between 1880 and 1914, parlour games were a particularly popular form of indoor amusement and this game of table-top quoits was enjoyed and played by all the family.

You will need

Fancy-ended cocktail stick

10mm diameter wooden washer bead

Four 8mm diameter metal jump rings

Enamel paints

Wood stain

Tacky glue

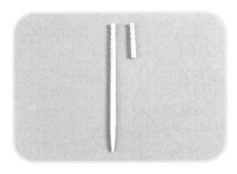

1 Using mitre cutters or a craft knife, begin by cutting the cocktail stick to ³/₄in long and carefully sand the end smooth using fine-grade sandpaper.

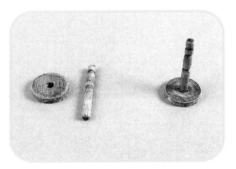

2 Stain the cocktail stick and wooden washer and leave to dry. Place the washer on a flat surface and glue the straight end of the cocktail stick into the washer hole, so that the end of the stick is flush with the underside of the washer.

3 Paint the metal jump rings in different colours with enamel paints (see Basic Techniques, page 12) and leave to dry.

Indoor Croquet Set

Mallet and ball games were played in Europe during the Middle Ages. The modern game of croquet emerged in Ireland and was introduced into England by John Jaques at the Great Exhibition in 1851. Croquet soon became fashionable amongst the middle classes, and was one of the first games that could be played by both sexes on an equal footing. This indoor version was just as popular and was played either on the floor or on a snooker (pool) table.

You will need

$^1/_{16}$in thick obechi sheet wood:
  1in x $^1/_2$in for box base
  two 1$^1/_8$in x $^1/_2$in for box sides
  two $^1/_2$in x $^1/_2$in for box ends
  1$^1/_8$in x $^5/_8$in for lid

$^1/_{32}$in thick obechi sheet wood,
1in x $^1/_2$in for inside lid

$^1/_8$in diameter hardwood dowel,
four $^3/_8$in lengths for mallet heads

$^3/_{64}$in diameter hardwood dowel:
  four $^7/_8$in lengths for mallet shafts
  $^3/_8$in length for winning post

3mm diameter metal washer bead

Cream tissue paper

24-gauge silver wire, 8in length

Twelve gold seed beads, size 11

$^3/_{16}$in diameter hardwood dowel for hoop mould

Four $^5/_{32}$in diameter ball bearings

Rope-coloured button thread

Wood stain

Enamel paints

Water-based acrylic paints

Tacky glue

1 Use fine-grade sandpaper to sand smooth any rough edges on all of the wooden components and then colour the wood pieces with a light-coloured wood stain such as antique pine or light oak (all except the winning post and hoop mould) – see Basic Techniques page 12 for using wood stain. Leave to dry.

2 Take the two box ends and transfer the hole positions from the template on page 62 on to the two pieces of wood. Drill holes through each piece using a $^1/_{32}$in drill bit. Thread the button thread through the holes in one of the end pieces and form a small loop. Place a mallet head piece between the loop and the wood to ensure that the two handles will be the same size. Knot the thread on the opposite side and trim neatly. Secure the knot with a dab of glue and remove the mallet head. Repeat the procedure with the other box end piece.

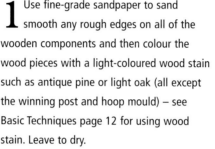

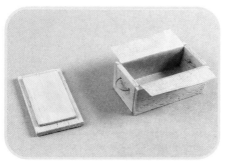

3 Glue the box sides and ends on to the outside edges of the box base, so that the base is sandwiched between, as shown.

4 Position the inside lid centrally on top of the lid and glue into place. Line the interior of the box with a 1in x 2in piece of cream tissue paper.

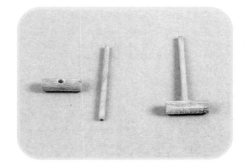

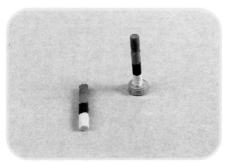

5 Take the four mallet heads and drill a hole centrally in each, drilling only part-way through the wood using a $^3/_{64}$in drill bit. Glue the mallet shafts into each of the holes.

6 Paint the winning post with blue, red, black and yellow water-based acrylic paints, as shown. Allow each level to dry before painting the next. Once dry, glue the end of the post into the washer bead.

7 Bend the end of the silver wire over a length of $^3/_{16}$in diameter hardwood dowel to form a hoop, then cut to $^1/_4$in high. Repeat until you have six hoops the same height. Glue the ends of the wire into a seed bead to enable the hoops to stand.

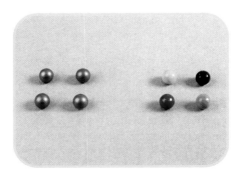

Variation

Roll $^5/_{32}$in diameter balls out of coloured polymer clay as an alternative to using ball bearings.

8 The balls are $^5/_{32}$in diameter ball bearings painted with enamel paints to match the colours on the winning post.

Bagatelle

Bagatelle is thought to have originated in France and is related to the pub games of billiards, pool and snooker. As with most pub games, smaller versions were invented that could be played at home and this version of bagatelle was particularly popular during the Victorian and Edwardian periods. Some bagatelles required the player to shoot the ball with a cue, whilst others had a sprung plunger. Obviously, playing with a cue relied more on the player's skill, whilst the sprung plunger introduced an element of luck.

You will need

$^1/_{16}$in thick obechi sheet wood, 2$^1/_2$in x 1$^1/_4$in for board

$^1/_{32}$in thick obechi sheet wood:
  2$^1/_2$in x 1$^1/_4$in for base
  10in x $^3/_{16}$in for outside rim

$^1/_{16}$in x $^1/_{16}$in obechi strip wood:
  1$^3/_4$in for start channel guide
  1$^1/_{16}$in for holder channel

$^3/_{64}$in diameter hardwood dowel, 1in length for cue

About ninety fine brass pins, $^1/_4$in length

Eight $^1/_{16}$in diameter ball bearings

Tweezers

Wood stain

Tacky glue

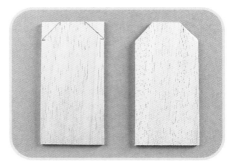

1 Taking the board and base obechi wood pieces, mark $^3/_8$in along from the corners at one short end on each piece of wood. Join the marks using a pencil and ruler and then remove the corner sections using either mitre cutters or a craft knife.

2 Place the board on top of the base and shape the two pieces together by rounding off the cuts with fine-grade sandpaper. Wipe wood stain sparingly over each side of the board and base and leave to dry (see Basic Techniques page 12).

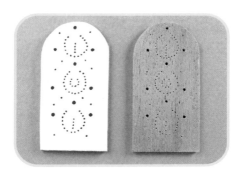

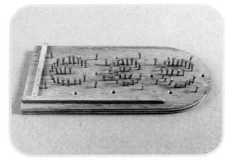

3 Transfer the bagatelle template (page 62) on to a piece of paper and attach to the board with tape. Using a $^1/_{16}$in drill bit, drill through the larger spots on the template and through the wood. Use a $^1/_{64}$in drill bit to puncture the small spots on the template into the wood. Remove the template. Glue the board on to the base, clamping or weighing it down while the glue dries.

4 Beginning with the inside of the loops, press the brass pins into place using tweezers. Taper the end of the starter channel guide piece using fine-grade sandpaper and then stain, along with the holder channel piece, and leave to dry. Glue on to the board as shown.

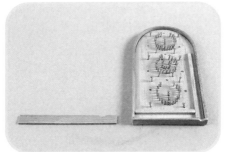

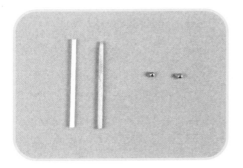

5 Stain the outside rim strip of wood and leave to dry. Cut off an 8in length and soak in warm water for ten minutes. Manipulate the wood with your hands carefully (to avoid splitting) to fit around the curved outside edge. Glue into position and clamp until dry. Remove excess wood using a craft knife and sand the ends in line with the straight end of the board.

6 Using a pin file or a folded piece of fine-grade sandpaper, carefully sand an indentation towards one end of the remaining outside strip of wood. Glue this against the straight end of the board, lining up the indentation with the start channel. Remove excess wood using a craft knife and sand the ends smooth. Stain the ends, along with the indentation to complete the game board.

7 Taper one end of the dowel using fine-grade sandpaper to make a cue and then stain. Place the cue into the starter channel and the ball bearings into the holder channel.

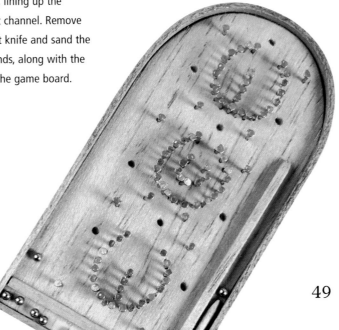

Draughts

Records show that variations of draughts (checkers) were played in ancient Egypt; the modern game, however, wasn't played in Europe until the 16th century. Nowadays, games are often categorized and draughts falls into the category of 'strategy games', as a player must use skill and intelligence to win. In draughts, each player starts with twelve counters and the aim is to capture all your opponent's pieces. Many board games, such as backgammon, are governed by the throw of a dice and are known as 'race games'.

You will need

$^1/_{16}$in thick obechi sheet wood, 1in x 1in for base

$^1/_{16}$in x $^1/_8$in obechi strip wood:
   two sides 1in
   two sides 1$^1/_8$in

Cocktail stick

White card for colour photocopying

Acrylic water-based paints

Shoe polish

Tacky glue

Variation

Make a backgammon board following the same instructions and colour photocopying the board on page 61. As this game needs thirty counters (fifteen black and fifteen white), four dice, and a doubling cube, it is recommended that just the board is made and displayed on a shelf.

1 Use fine-grade sandpaper to sand smooth any rough edges on all of the wooden components. Use shoe polish to colour the side wood pieces and one side of the base. See Basic Techniques page 12 for using colouring mediums.

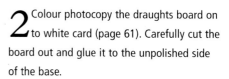

2 Colour photocopy the draughts board on to white card (page 61). Carefully cut the board out and glue it to the unpolished side of the base.

3 Place the short side wood pieces opposite each other and glue on to the outside edges of the base. Glue the longer side pieces on to the remaining outside edges.

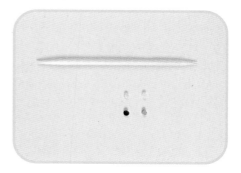

4 Make enough counters to show a game in play by slicing a cocktail stick into pieces about $^1/_{16}$in thick using a mitre block and saw. Sand and paint the counters black or ivory using acrylic paints. Glue the pieces on the black squares on the board.

Outdoor
Toys and Games

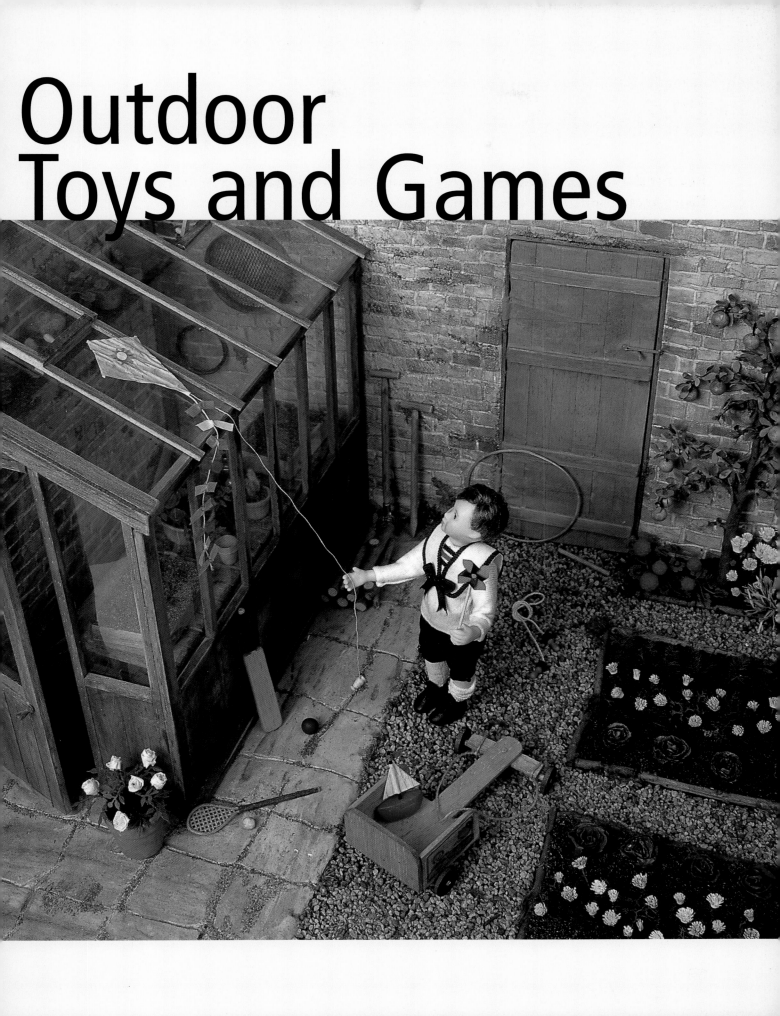

Skipping Rope and Hoop

Before the 19th century skipping ropes did not have handles, and were basically old clothes'-line or rope knotted at each end. Wooden handles were added to make the rope easier to hold and in poor industrial areas they were made from bobbins from the cotton mills.

Traditionally, hoops were between one and four feet in diameter, and were hit with a stick whilst rolling along the ground. Children without toy hoops would make do with an iron ring from beer barrels.

You will need

For the skipping rope

Two natural round wooden beads 4mm diameter for handle

Two 14mm wooden belaying pins for handles

Cream button thread, 6in length for rope

Water-based acrylic paints

Tacky glue

For the hoop and stick

Centre (reed) cane size 00, 6in length for hoop

Cocktail stick, 1in long

Aluminium tape or foil, ³⁄₈in x ³⁄₈in

Wood stain

Tacky glue

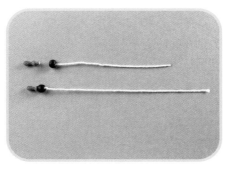

To make the skipping rope:

1 Paint the wooden beads and belaying pins using water-based acrylic paint. Once dry, use mitre cutters to trim the straight end on the belaying pins to ³⁄₁₆in.

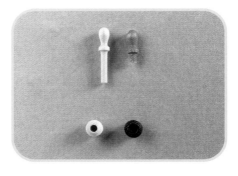

2 Place one end of the button thread into the painted wooden bead. Dab a tiny amount of tacky glue on the straight end of the belaying pin and press into the bead so that the end of the thread is caught inside. Repeat with the other end of the rope.

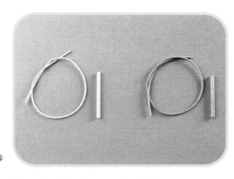

To make the hoop and stick:

1 Sand the ends of the cocktail stick using fine-grade sandpaper. Colour the stick and the length of centre cane with a light wood stain, such as antique pine or light oak, so that the hoop and stick look well used.

2 Soak the centre cane in warm water for a few minutes, shake off any excess water and bend into a circle. Hold the ends together and wrap around some aluminium tape or foil smeared with tacky glue. Ask someone to hold the cane whilst you do this. Leave to dry.

Windmill

Early manuscripts reveal that wooden windmill sails fixed to sticks date back to medieval times and show boys and girls at play with windmills. Paper windmills were available during the Edwardian era and became particularly popular because they were cheap and bright. Some had a piece of metal fixed between the stick and the paper so that when the sails revolved they made a whirring sound.

You will need

Coloured paper

Fibre-tip pen in a contrasting colour

Centre (reed) cane size 000, 1¼in length

Paper punch, ¹⁄₁₆in diameter circle

Tacky glue

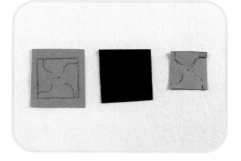

1 Transfer the windmill template (page 62) on to a piece of coloured paper. Colour the underside of the paper with a contrasting-coloured fibre-tipped pen and leave to dry for a few minutes. Cut out the pattern with small, sharp scissors and snip along the inner lines.

2 Place the windmill on a flat surface, pen-coloured side down. Using the tip of a cocktail stick, bring the flaps into the centre of the windmill one by one, dabbing a spot of tacky glue on each time to hold in place.

Variation

If you have a dolls' house toyshop, make an effective display of windmills by using a variety of coloured paper and fibre-tipped pens.

3 Cut a ¹⁄₁₆in diameter circle out of your original coloured paper either by hand or using a ¹⁄₁₆in circle paper punch. Glue the circle to the centre of the windmill.

4 To make the stick soak the centre cane in warm water for a few minutes, weigh down each end after pulling straight and leave to dry. Glue one end of the straightened centre cane on the back of the windmill.

Tennis Racket and Ball

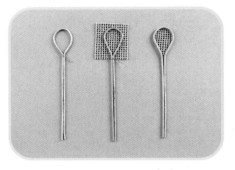

Versions of the game of tennis can be dated back to ancient times, however, the game that was more like the tennis we know today was played in the French monasteries during the 10th century. The first Wimbledon lawn tennis championships took place in England in 1879 and as the years progressed, so did the game's popularity around the world. Middle class children used this child's tennis racket and ball during games lessons at school and at home during the Victorian and Edwardian years.

You will need

Centre (reed) cane size 00, 6in length

Brown tapestry canvas (18 holes to the inch), $^3/_4$in square piece

Brown floral tape, 2in x $^1/_4$in strip

34-gauge jewellery wire, $1^1/_2$in length

2mm diameter round bead

White toilet or face tissue

Wood stain

Tacky glue

1 Stain the centre cane and soak in warm water for a few minutes until pliable. Shake to remove excess water and fold in half to form a loop. Place on top of the tennis racket template (page 62) and manoeuvre the cane to the size and shape of the racket head. Straighten the ends to make a handle.

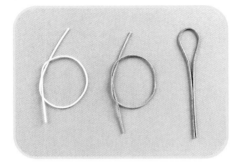

2 Wind jewellery wire around the base of the racket head to hold the shape whilst the cane is drying. Run a small amount of glue over one side of the racket head, press down on top of the tapestry canvas and leave to dry. Remove the wire and trim excess canvas with small, sharp scissors.

3 Trim any excess cane on the handle so that the full length of the racket is $1^7/_8$in. Rub some glue along the trimmed handle and wind around the brown floral tape, starting immediately below the racket head.

4 To make a cloth-covered tennis ball, roll a 2mm bead in tacky glue. Place this on a single layer of tissue and with the smallest amount of tacky glue on your fingers roll into a ball. To create a well-used tennis ball, roll on top of a used tea bag and leave to dry.

Cricket Bat and Ball

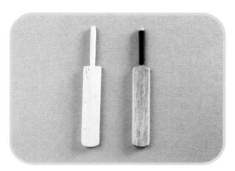

Versions of cricket can be traced back to the Middle Ages but it wasn't until the middle of the 18th century that it became an established sport. During the Victorian and Edwardian eras many boys played cricket at their preparatory or public schools and continued to play the game during their leisure time. To actually possess your own bat at this time was an eager young boy's dream.

You will need

$^3/_{32}$in thick obechi sheet wood, $2^1/_4$in x $^5/_{16}$in

Black acrylic paint

Black cotton thread, 24in length

Light brown shoe polish

Burgundy polymer clay

Tacky glue

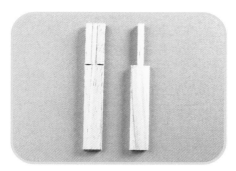

1 Transfer the cricket bat template (page 62) on to your wood and use mitre cutters or a craft knife to cut out the shape. To avoid the wood splitting, first cut against the grain at the bottom of the handle and then cut along the length of the handle.

2 Use fine-grade sandpaper to shape and sand smooth. Rub light brown shoe polish over the bat, then buff up using a clean cloth. Paint the handle with black water-based acrylic paint and leave to dry.

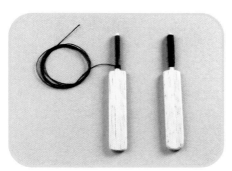

3 Cover the handle with a thin layer of tacky glue and, starting at the base, wind black cotton neatly around, working your way up the handle.

4 Make a cricket ball by rolling out a $^3/_{16}$in diameter ball of burgundy polymer clay. Harden by baking in an oven, following the manufacturer's instructions.

Go-cart

Larger outdoor toys became popular towards the end of the Victorian years, and in particular those that offered some excitement. Go-carts, mostly home-made from wooden boxes and perambulator (baby carriage) wheels, were an excellent stand-in if you weren't able to afford a bicycle. Children spent many hours racing each another down hills. The go-cart in this project does not have moving wheels.

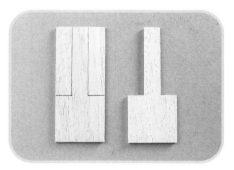

You will need

$^{1}/_{16}$in thick obechi sheet wood:
  $2^{3}/_{4}$in x $1^{1}/_{8}$in for base
  $1^{1}/_{4}$in x $^{3}/_{4}$in for back (grain to run
  with shortest length)
  two $1^{1}/_{8}$in x $^{5}/_{8}$in for sides
  two $1^{1}/_{8}$in x $^{1}/_{4}$in for axle holders

Two cocktail sticks

Four 10mm wooden washer beads

Fine brass pin, $^{1}/_{4}$in length

Cream button thread, 8in length

White paper for colour photocopying

Wood stain

Silver enamel paint

Tacky glue

1 Take the back piece of wood, mark $^{1}/_{8}$in from the corners on one long side. Join the marks, then remove the two corners using either mitre cutters or a craft knife. Round off using fine-grade sandpaper.

2 Transfer the go-cart template (page 62) on to the base piece of wood and cut out. To avoid the wood splitting, first cut against the grain at the front of the seat and then along the length of the leg rest.

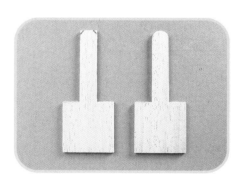

3 Mark $^{1}/_{16}$in from each corner at the narrow end. Join the marks with a pencil and ruler, remove the corners and round off with sandpaper as before.

4 Take a side wood piece and mark $1/8$in from one corner. Join the marks, remove the corner and round off as before. Repeat with the remaining side wood piece. Sand any remaining wooden components and wipe wood stain over each piece. The wooden washer beads can either be stained or painted with water-based acrylic paint.

5 Place the base on a flat surface and glue the sides and back to the outside edges of the base as shown. Colour photocopy the advertisements on page 61 on to white paper, wipe over with a light stain to mimic age, cut out and glue to each side of the cart.

6 Make the wheel axles by cutting two cocktail sticks to $1^1/2$in each and glue a wooden washer bead to each end. Turn the go-cart upside-down, mark $1/4$in from the seat end and glue the axle holder next to this line. Glue an axle on the axle holder.

7 With a pencil make a mark centrally $3/16$in from the tip of the cart. Glue an axle holder to an axle and place under the tip of the cart so that a hole drilled through will continue into the axle. Drill the hole using a $1/64$in drill bit. Attach the front wheels by pressing the brass pin into the drilled hole.

8 Make a rope handle by attaching each end of the button thread to the front axle section of the cart and knotting underneath as shown. Dab a tiny amount of tacky glue where the threads meet and once dry trim excess thread with small, sharp scissors.

9 Paint the ends of the cocktail sticks with silver enamel paint to look like hubcaps. To finish, paint the brass pin head silver.

57

Kite

It is thought that kites originated in China around the 3rd century BC, where they had a ritualistic or religious significance. Kites have been made in all shapes and sizes, either ready-made, home-made or as a kit, and instructions exist on how to make one from as early as 1405. Kites have provided hours of fascination to adults and children of all classes, for many centuries.

You will need

Paper ribbon in contrasting colours

Medium-thickness card

Cream cotton thread, 14in length

Cream button thread, 3in length

Centre (reed) cane size 000, 5in length

6mm single column or $^3/_8$in length of cocktail stick

Paper punches, mini sun and $^1/_8$in diameter circle

Tacky glue

1 Transfer the kite template on page 62 on to a piece of medium-thickness card. Lay the template on top of your paper ribbon (the creases running with the length of the kite) and cut around the kite shape.

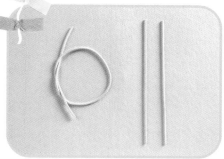

2 Soak the centre cane in warm water for a few minutes, weigh down each end after pulling straight. Once dry, cut into two lengths of $2^1/_2$in.

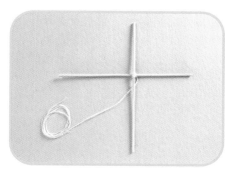

3 Form a cross with the two pieces of centre cane and wind one end of the cotton thread over and around the middle of the cross to secure the shape. Knot the end to secure but don't trim the excess cotton.

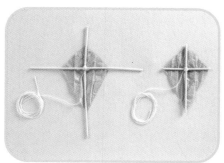

4 Lay the cane cross on the paper kite, aligning the corners of the kite with the frame and glue into place. Trim any excess cane with small, sharp scissors once the glue has dried.

5 Wind the excess cotton from the kite frame around the centre of the single barrel (or cocktail stick), dabbing tiny amounts of tacky glue every now and then to ensure that the cotton stays in place. Leave about 1in of unwound cotton between the kite and the string barrel.

6 Decorate the front of the kite with shapes punched out of contrasting coloured paper ribbon.

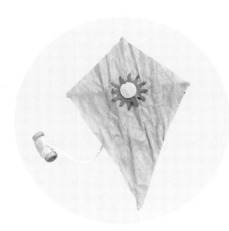

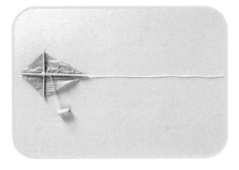

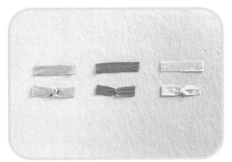

7 To form the tail, place the kite face down and glue one end of the button thread on to the kite frame as shown.

8 Cut about nine pieces of paper ribbon $\frac{1}{8}$in x $\frac{1}{2}$in (with creases running with the longest length of the paper). Hold the ends of each strip of paper ribbon, then twist each one once, to form a bow.

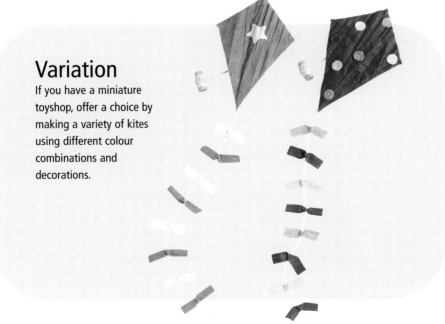

9 Place the kite face up on a non-porous work surface. Position the bows at regular intervals on top of the kite's tail and then glue on to the button thread. Once totally dry, lift the kite's tail and attached bows carefully off the work surface.

Variation
If you have a miniature toyshop, offer a choice by making a variety of kites using different colour combinations and decorations.

Sailing Boat

Toy boats have been objects of play for centuries and were originally replicas of full-sized boats made by the owners out of the same materials. This boat is based on the simply designed wooden basin boat which was extremely popular during the Edwardian period. At that time it was fashionable to dress both boys and girls in sailor suits, and a child so-dressed, with a toy boat tucked under their arm, was a common sight.

You will need

¹/₄in x ¹/₄in obechi strip wood, ³/₄in length

Centre (reed) cane size 00, ⁷/₈in length

Paper ribbon in two contrasting colours

Enamel paints

Tacky glue

Variation

Make two smaller versions of the same boat using a ⁵/₈in length of ³/₁₆in x ³/₁₆in strip wood and a ³/₈in length of ¹/₈in x ¹/₈in strip wood. Alter the sizes of the masts and sails accordingly.

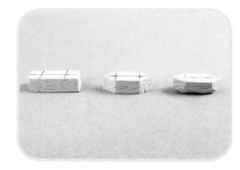

1 Take the wood block and using a pencil mark ³/₁₆in from each end and then ¹/₈in across the width of the wood. Using the marks as your guide, cut off the corners and begin to carve the block into the hull of a boat using a craft knife. Shape and smooth with fine-grade sandpaper.

2 Mark the centre of the deck and use a ³/₆₄in drill bit to drill a hole about ¹/₈in deep. To make the mast, soak the centre cane in warm water for a few minutes, weigh down each end after pulling straight and leave to dry. Paint the hull and mast with enamel paints (see Basic Techniques page 12).

3 The large sail is made from paper ribbon ³/₄in x ¹/₂in, with the creases running with the width of the paper. Fold the piece in half then cut out the shape as shown in the picture, and glue to the mast.

4 Make the small sail from two pieces of paper ribbon ⁷/₁₆in x ¹/₄in (creases lengthways). Shape as before and glue each side of the mast. For a flag, cut ¹/₁₆in x ³/₈in paper ribbon, shape one end and glue around the mast. Glue the mast into the deck hole.

Templates

Reproduce colour templates either by colour photocopying or by scanning into a computer and printing out on photo-quality card or paper.

Number Cubes

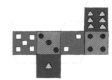

Jumping Jacks

Draughts Board

Go-cart Advertising Signs

Picture Bricks

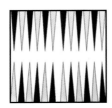

Backgammon Board

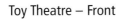

Toy Theatre – Front

Toy Theatre – Top

Toy Theatre – Backdrop

Toy Theatre – Figures

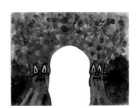

Toy Theatre – Scenes

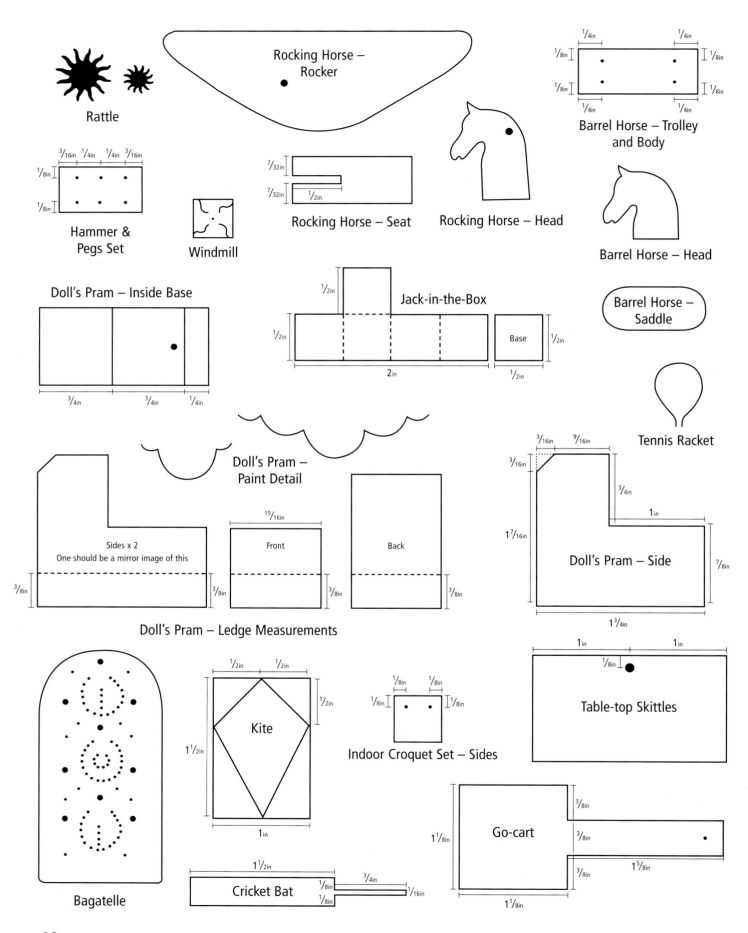

Rattle

Rocking Horse – Rocker

Barrel Horse – Trolley and Body

Hammer & Pegs Set

Windmill

Rocking Horse – Seat

Rocking Horse – Head

Barrel Horse – Head

Doll's Pram – Inside Base

Jack-in-the-Box

Base

Barrel Horse – Saddle

Tennis Racket

Doll's Pram – Paint Detail

Sides x 2
One should be a mirror image of this

Front

Back

Doll's Pram – Side

Doll's Pram – Ledge Measurements

Kite

Indoor Croquet Set – Sides

Table-top Skittles

Bagatelle

Cricket Bat

Go-cart

Suppliers

UK

Bead Exclusive
Nixon House,
119-121 Teignmouth Road,
Torquay, Devon TQ1 4HA
tel: 01803 322000
www.beadexclusive.com
beads & jewellery findings

Buttons 'n' Badges
4 Buckingham Road, Poynton,
Cheshire SK12 1JH
tel: 01625 873117
*wooden beads, belaying pins, single
columns, centre cane (reed cane), paper
ribbon, stamens & craft picks*

Dolls House Holidays
Wells Cottage, 204 Main Road,
Milford, Stafford ST17 0UN
tel: 01785 664659
mitre cutters

Evie's Crafts
79 Dale Street, Milnrow,
Rochdale, Lancashire OL16 3NJ
tel: 01706 712489
paper punches & quilling paper

Jennifer's of Walsall
51 George Street, Walsall,
West Midlands WS1 1RS
tel: 01922 623382
*obechi wood, bass wood, hardware,
polymer clay & tools*

Jojays
Moore Road,
Bourton-on-the-Water,
Gloucestershire, GL54 2AZ
tel: 01451 810081
www.jojays.co.uk
hardware, tools, leather & glue

Katy Sue Dolls
Unit 201
Tedco, Henry Robson Way,
South Shields,
Tyne & Wear NE33 1RF
tel: 0191 427 4571
www.katysuedolls.com
dolls

Macc Model Engineers Supplies
45A Saville Street,
Macclesfield, Cheshire SK11 7LQ
tel: 01625 433938
ball bearings

Wood Supplies
Monkey Puzzle Cottage,
53 Woodmansterne Lane,
Wallington, Surrey SM6 0SW
tel: 020 8669 7266 (evenings)
jelutong wood

US

Cane and Reed
Box 762, Manchester,
CT 06045
tel: 800-646-6586
www.caneandreed.com
centre cane (round reed cane)

Dick Blick Art Materials
PO Box 1267, Galesburg,
IL 61402-1267
tel: 800-828-4548
www.dickblick.com
*tools, paper punches, polymer clay, craft
picks & paper ribbon*

General Bead
317 National City Blvd.
National City CA 91950-1110
tel: 1-619-336-0100
www.genbead.com
beads & jewellery findings

Happy Hobby Shop
7125 N. 76th Street,
Milwaukee WI 53223
tel: 414-461-6013
www.happyhobby.com
tools, glue & bass wood

Nature Coast Hobbies, Inc.
6773 S. Hancock Road,
Homosassa Florida 34448
tel: 352-628-3990
www.naturecoast.com
belaying pins, single columns & tools

Rose's Doll House
12750 W. Capitol Drive
Brookfield, WI 53005
tel: 262-373-0350
www.happyhobby.com
hardware & tools

Index

abacus 15
aluminium foil and
    tape 10
aluminium tube 10

backgammon 50
bagatelle 48–9
barrel horse 26–7
bass wood 8
belaying pin 10
blackboard 18–19
boat 60
brick truck 34
bricks 14, 17
brushes 9
building blocks 14
bunka 10, 12

cart 56–7
centre cane 10
chalk 19
chamfering 12
checkers 50
clown 42
craft pick 10
cricket bat and ball 55
croquet, indoor 46–7
cutting wood 12

devil among the tailors 44
Dickens, Charles 40
distressing 12
doll 42
dolls' pram 32–3
draughts 50

easel 18–19
enamel paints 9, 12

farm animals 28–9
floral tape 10

gilt cream 9
glove puppets 38–9
glues 9
go-cart 56–7

hammer and pegs 20
hoop and stick 52
horses 24–8
houses 14

imperial measurements 7

Jack-in-the-box 40–1
jelutong wood 8
jewellery findings 11
jumping Jack 22

kite 58–9

lampshade fringing
    see bunka

mailcart 32–3
materials and equipment 8–11
metal, painting 12
metallic paste 9
metric conversion chart 7
mitring 8, 12

number cubes 22

obechi wood 8

paints 9, 12
paper punch 9
paper ribbon 11
paper toys 22
picture bricks 17
pin file 8
pin vice 8
polymer clay 11
poupard 21

Punch and Judy 38–9
puppet theatre and
    puppets 38–9

quilling paper 11
quoits, table-top 45

rattle 21
rocking horse 24–5

safety tips 11
sailing boat 60
sheep on wheels 28–9
shoe polish 9, 12
single columns 11
skipping rope 52
skittles, table-top 44
Steiff, Margaret 28

tapestry canvas 11
templates, using 12
tennis racket and ball 54
theatres
    puppet 38–9
    toy 36–7
tools 8–9
towing pin 29
toyshops 6
train set 30–1
truck 34

Victorian period 6

windmill 53
wire 11
wood stain 9, 12

xylophone 16

About the author

Jane Harrop started making miniatures as a hobby nine years ago, when she made and demonstrated the projects at her local miniatures club. Her enthusiasm turned this hobby into her job – she has been teaching adult education classes on making miniatures for the past six years, and has had articles published in *Dolls' House World* magazine. Jane sells her work through local miniatures fairs to collectors and also presents miniature workshops. Jane is married with two daughters, and lives in Cheshire, UK.

Acknowledgments

Thank you to the following people and organizations that have assisted in making this project book possible.
Brian Gordon for the artwork. Katy Sue Dolls for their dolls (details in Suppliers). Alan Denwood and Bob Williams for their support and advice. Terry and Peter Ablett for their xylophone design. The Museum of Childhood, Bethnal Green, London for historical information.